HAUNTED FLORIDA GHOST TOWNS

HEATHER LEIGH, PhD

Haunted America

Published by Haunted America
A Division of The History Press
Charleston, SC
www.historypress.com

Front cover: Desert Inn Bar and Restaurant after it was struck twice by tractor trailers. *Aidan Carroll-Landon.*

First published 2024

Manufactured in the United States

ISBN 9781467156479

Library of Congress Control Number: 2023948363

To my godfather, William Geeraerts (Uncle Bill)
You always believed in me, and I am forever grateful for that.

CONTENTS

FOREWORD

Ghost towns in Florida? What are ghost towns anyway? Why does a once bustling community suddenly become abandoned? And in Florida, where growth never ends, why are towns left to die all alone? Are all "ghost towns" haunted? This book by Heather Leigh Carroll-Landon, PhD, explains these questions in detail.

From its border with Louisiana to the famous Keys, Florida has a unique, diverse and sometimes tragic background. Initially viewed as a frontier land where futures could be realized, it became the epitome of sun and fun. It's a true vacation paradise. Looking for citrus, sun and sandy beaches, tourists and vacationers arrived from across the United States and the world to enjoy all of the hospitality the Sunshine State had to offer. Yet despite this cheery façade, Florida's history paints a picture of struggle and anguish, where the will to survive is the only thing the early settlers had to hold on to. These early pioneers made their homes amid mosquito-infected swamps, wild animals and tropical heat. An inhospitable land that many were not accustomed to and sometimes never became acclimated to. But it wasn't always the land and the climate that made moving to Florida difficult.

Florida was a wild state where lawlessness ruled in many areas, and only the strongest in mind and spirit survived. Florida often had a less-than-desirable reputation, from the pirates, bandits and scoundrels of the eighteenth and nineteenth centuries to the bootleggers and smugglers of the Prohibition era. Yet despite this, those desiring to conquer this untamed land and build a true paradise kept coming within it. Those early settlers knew that they would succeed in building a future in paradise. And as history has proven, they did succeed and prosper more often than not.

As soon as they begin to read *Haunted Florida Ghost Towns*, readers will be transported back to that time in Florida's history most people today do not realize existed. Hidden in the pages of this book, the reader will recognize how difficult it was to survive and prosper in old Florida. Heather Leigh's ability to send the reader back to that innocent, yet often violent, day in the history of the Sunshine State is remarkable. The fact that there are abandoned ghost towns in Florida stands in contrast to the state's reputation of amusement parks, citrus groves, sunny beaches and warm winters. She also explains that not all ghost towns are haunted but abandoned by most, if not all, of the townsfolk that lived there. While reading *Haunted Florida Ghost Towns*, the reader will find there is so much more to Florida than meets the eye, and Heather Leigh has done an excellent job of expressing that!

In addition to learning more about Florida's past, we find that the consequence of towns being abandoned is that sometimes their spirits decide never to leave. It also becomes clear to the reader that it isn't only the buildings on the land that are haunted but the land itself. With the violent events that took place back in old Florida, is there any wonder that the land itself absorbed some of that energy? These stories fuel the mystery of what exists on the other side of the veil of life as we know it.

Heather Leigh shares accounts from all over the state, and those stories are compelling and, at times, chilling. Only some authors can share the detailed history and, simultaneously, weave the legends and tales of the paranormal into that history the way she does. The reader will not only become more familiar with the ghostly occurrences of the Sunshine State but will also leave with a better understanding of what it took to build Florida into what it is today.

Heather Leigh has earned a solid reputation for her research and the ability to share that with the reader. *Haunted Florida Ghost Towns* continues this tradition. This is a book that leaves the reader wanting to learn more. And isn't that what exploration of the unknown is all about? Enjoy.

—Larry Lawson

ACKNOWLEDGEMENTS

My paranormal team, Exploration Paranormal, was created to assist those needing help with hauntings, educate others and help keep the memory of haunted locations alive. Joined by my husband and son—Josh and Aidan—I am forever grateful they help me with theories and research.

I also want to thank Larry Lawson of the Florida Bureau of Paranormal Investigations for writing an amazing foreword. I am looking forward to working with you on projects in the future.

INTRODUCTION

The term *ghost towns* brings to mind communities from the Old West where there were once bustling boom towns but today are abandoned and lonely pieces to the puzzles of the past.

With this image ingrained into a person's mind, it is challenging to visualize ghost towns with sandy beaches and palm trees swaying in the wind.

A little-known fact about Florida is it is home to more than 250 ghost towns, many of which remain the home for the spirits of former inhabitants, Civil War deserters, pirates and more. These towns are quickly vanishing from Florida's landscape, and through paranormal research, we can fill in the gaps between the living present and the dead past. By investigating and preserving these abandoned towns, we can build that bridge between Florida's historical past and the present.

Haunted Florida Ghost Towns covers the many abandoned locations in the Sunshine State where paranormal entities are known to roam.

Take a journey into the world of the supernatural and learn the history behind why Florida has so many ghost towns and the energy that remains to fuel paranormal activity.

1

WHAT MAKES A GHOST TOWN IN FLORIDA?

Florida is not the first state that comes to mind when discussing ghost towns; however, it is one of the top states on the East Coast of the United States in number of ghost towns. Ghost towns in Florida are similar to those in the West and are subject to the same classifications:

Abandoned Ghost Town
Working Ghost Town
Near Ghost Town

According to the website Western Mining History, a ghost town is "an abandoned village, town or city."[1] Often a town becomes a ghost town when the area's economic activity has slowed or failed. Additionally, natural or human-caused disasters—massacres, uncontrolled lawlessness, government actions, floods, disease or, as many Florida ghost towns experienced, hurricanes—can create ghost towns Ultimately, these towns were once thriving, and then suddenly, the community's purpose no longer exists, forcing residents to leave to find a way to support themselves and their families.

An "abandoned ghost town" is one where there are no residents and Mother Nature has left the town to ruin or be overtaken. In some cases, abandoned ghost towns have been purchased, preserved and kept by individuals or private organizations but remain with zero residents.

A "working ghost town" is one where a handful of residents, often fewer than one to two hundred, still work in the community doing their best to help maintain the ghost town's relevance. Often in working ghost towns, the residents survive on catering to tourists and those wanting to catch a glimpse of Florida's past.

A "near ghost town" is a community that may still have a significant population, but it is not what it used to be many years ago. A hypothetical example of a near ghost town is if Disney were to leave Central Florida, and the population went down to about one thousand residents.

These classifications fit many of the ghost towns in Florida, including those featured in this book. In some rare situations, ghost towns have been revived by new community endeavors and transformed into a new, bustling community. But this situation is scarce, especially in some of the more remote areas of the Sunshine State.

Today, most ghost towns have remnants of buildings and structures, and most have a town cemetery, often in less desirable condition. More than 250 ghost towns in Florida provide many opportunities to explore and dive deep into the Sunshine State's historical past.

Many of Florida's towns were founded on natural resources, such as lakes, rivers, the Gulf of Mexico and the Atlantic Ocean. Natural resources provided residents with everything they needed to survive and thrive as Florida began its journey through time. As small towns appeared on the map, residents took advantage of natural resources. They relied heavily on fishing, lumber, phosphate, citrus, clams, oysters, watermelons and other land and sea products. The abundance of these resources created a boom in Florida communities, similar to how the gold rush caused a boom in western states.

The Florida economy was hit hard during the Great Depression in 1929, and many small towns started dwindling in population, resulting

Careyville, Northern Florida. The houses have been deserted since the mill closed. *Dorthea Lange, Library of Congress.*

in the number of ghost towns we see today. Additionally, hurricanes and unexpected freezes during some of the coldest winters on record caused many residents to flee their coastal communities to seek a better life outside of the Sunshine State.

Some towns experienced the start of their demise when the railroads shut down during the Great Depression and highways were built to bypass these small towns. Other towns suffered losses during the various gold rushes, when many residents departed Florida communities for a chance to strike it rich, leaving towns abandoned to time before the West ever learned what a ghost town was.

The unique thing about living in or visiting Florida is when you drive around, there is a great chance you will encounter a sign or historical marker. These signs and markers identify the area's historical significance, sharing details of events, activities and facts about the past. If you see one of these historical markers when driving through Florida, do not keep driving. Take the time to stop and learn a little bit more about what went into the making of what Florida is today.

2
WHY ARE FLORIDA GHOST TOWNS HAUNTED?

When many people think of Florida, they automatically think about the Central Florida area, full of theme parks and family-friendly fun. Others may think about the beautiful beaches and amazing oceanside communities offering fabulous shopping, dining and entertainment opportunities.

It is most likely the last thing people think of (unless you are a paranormal researcher) is the hidden parts of the Sunshine State that have been abandoned and left to ruin. These ghost towns are home to creaky old buildings and structures covered in vines, boarded-up churches and derelict houses. Plus, these abandoned communities contain eerie cemeteries, enhancing these towns' creepy feel.

There are numerous Florida ghost towns, and though humans have abandoned them, several remain occupied by spirits, creepy-crawlies and unknown supernatural and cryptozoological beings.

During the 1800s and into the early 1900s, small towns across Florida were centered on farming and sawmills. Several of these towns were established along railways and near orange groves, so the residents had plenty of steady work. However, extreme weather conditions and catastrophes, such as hurricanes, floods and freezes, brought these lively towns to a screeching halt. When the town's purpose vanished, the residents soon left to find bigger and better things.

Today, Florida ghost towns and abandoned estates are only a small reminder of what life was like during this time. Several ghost towns today have overgrown graveyards and legends that will give even the most experienced paranormal researcher the heebie-jeebies.

So, how do ghost towns in one of the fastest-growing states in the United States develop and become overrun with paranormal activity? One explanation is that these towns have been abandoned and left isolated from the rest of the world so that, like the overgrowth of vegetation, spirits, cryptids and other paranormal entities have found a home where the living are most likely to leave them alone.

Though not always the reason, some believe that if a traumatic event occurred at a property or someone died there, there is a greater chance of it being haunted. The more we learn about the paranormal, this reason is becoming less and less common, especially as other theories and ideas are introduced to this field of research.

Another reason why ghost towns become haunted is the former residents loved living there, and despite having to leave their homes, that is where they felt the happiest and most comfortable. Many spirits prefer to return to a place in the afterlife where they are happy. When they were booming, Florida's ghost towns were lively places where families settled down; business owners found success, and communities came together.

When faced with tragedy, such as devastation and destruction caused by hurricanes, floods, mischievous behavior, war or attacks by local Indian tribes, residents were forced to leave their happy communities and, in the afterlife, return to rejoice in the memories of their once happy life.

In some situations, today's ghost towns in Florida were created by residents being forced out by the government or big corporations. These towns were their homes, and it is believed that because they can go back in the afterlife, many spirits still linger in these abandoned communities.

Many theories could explain why Florida ghost towns are haunted and popular hiding places for spirits. Another possibility is that some spirits may be attached to the items left behind or put on display in nearby museums, chambers of commerce and homes of the few remaining residents. Things that may contain attachments include antiques, structures, tools, toys, jewelry and clothing.

Another possible cause of paranormal activity in Florida's ghost towns is the theory behind psychic imprints on the land and objects causing residual hauntings. These residual energies essentially develop when a person conducts the same activity day after day, week after week, month after month or year after year. With the repetition of the activity, the energy of the person conducting the activity becomes imprinted on the environment. Over time, this energy plays back at the same time and frequency the original activity occurred, causing what many researchers believe to be paranormal activity when essentially it is just the energy playing itself out over time—similar to a song put on repeat.

The possibilities of why ghost towns are haunted presented in this chapter are just the beginning of the many theories paranormal researchers have regarding why spirits and other supernatural entities remain behind to haunt a location. This book covers the many haunted areas in Florida, possible reasons behind why they are haunted and the entities that have decided to live eternity in these ghost towns.

3

ARE ALL FLORIDA GHOST TOWNS HAUNTED?

Not all ghost towns are haunted. Still, there may be some logical explanations as to why not everyone experiences paranormal activity in ghost towns or why no significant amounts of paranormal incidents are reported.

One of the most common reasons not everyone encounters a spirit while visiting a Florida ghost town is that they may not be open to the idea. As we grow older, we are often told ghosts are not real and, over time, close our minds and hearts to the possibilities within the supernatural realm. Because we close ourselves off to the possibilities, we either do not notice paranormal activity or the spirits pick up on our denial of the afterlife and choose to stay in the shadows.

Another possible reason why some Florida ghost towns may have no reports of paranormal activity is because the few residents still living there, those who work there and visitors are so busy with their daily lives, activities and routines that they don't notice or are unaware of anything paranormal occurring around them. It is also possible that people in these towns do not have the time to see what is happening around them.

Additionally, there is the possibility that many residents and visitors are encountering paranormal entities but do not believe what they see and move on with life. Or they fear if they were to share their story with others they would think they were crazy. So instead, these experiences and encounters go unreported and no one knows the truth behind paranormal activity in some of Florida's ghost towns.

Some of the ghost towns in Florida are out of the way and it is challenging to get there, which makes for very few visitors. Because some cities lack people visiting, no one is there to witness, document or monitor paranormal activity. Ultimately, this does not mean these towns do not have ghosts, spirits, cryptids or other supernatural beings. Their presence has simply not yet been identified, witnessed and documented.

Finally, one of the reasons why there might be no paranormal activity in a ghost town is because the spirits don't want to be discovered. They simply want to live in the afterlife undisturbed and alone. Paranormal entities are not circus animals and do not communicate, interact or appear on command. Even if a paranormal researcher is trying to make contact, there is no guarantee that spirits will make themselves known if there are any present.

These are only some reasons why some Florida ghost towns are not haunted (or appear not haunted). As there are many reasons why these towns have spirits, there are just as many reasons why they may not be haunted.

4
ANONA

Anona was discovered in 1883 when Captain John Thomas Lowe made a water landing in the area and created a makeshift port. This port allowed commerce to flow from Key West to Anona, which continued to grow and thrive around the landing. At first, the town was named Lowe's Landing, but the postmaster from Cedar Key suggested it be named Anona, after the sweet apples available from Key West.

In December 1883, Jefferson Lowe was named postmaster of Anona's new post office, and the town boomed shortly after. A railroad spur was constructed to cross over the island allowing for the transportation of goods to and from the community. The bridge was removed in 1928.

Eventually, the town's post office was converted to a general store, and in 1872, residents built the town's first church, with Reverend John Wells as its preacher. One year later, the city formed a church board, and it was determined the church's building would be used for a schoolhouse to operate on weekdays. In 1900, the school was moved to a new building.

A second church was built in 1882, and the remaining residents still use this structure today.

Despite the town's flourishing activity, over time, residents of Anona dispersed, leaving the community, with many moving into the Largo area. Eventually, the city was absorbed into Largo.

Today, Anona remains home to a church and cemetery that receive many visitors yearly. Several visitors have witnessed apparitions, shadow figures and other unexplained activity around the church grounds and lurking in the graveyard. There are reports of apparitions with glowing white eyes appearing a few feet away on nights when there is a full moon.

Is Anona haunted? If one dares to walk the cemetery and visit the church, they may find the answers—or come face to face with the glowing-eyed creature lurking in the town's shadows.

5
ATSENA OTIE KEY

Atsena Otie Key is a community known for its creepy cemetery, but only a few know the historical past. This ghost town hides among the shadows. From 1818 to the early 1820s, the island was a trading post location, a vital spot during the First Seminole War. After the war, it remained a trading post until 1821, when Florida became a U.S. territory.[2]

The commander of the U.S. troops, General Walker Keith Armistead, ordered a hospital to be constructed on the island in 1840 during the Second Seminole War. In 1842, Colonel William J. Worth, the U.S. Army commander of Florida, negotiated an agreement with Seminole leaders on the island known as Depot Key. The Seminoles agreed to retreat to the southernmost areas of Florida. The army would leave them alone in exchange, and the colonel declared the Second Seminole War was over.

A few months later, Depot Key was struck by a hurricane that caused vast amounts of damage, forcing the army to abandon the post on the island.

Shortly after, more settlers came to the area and called it Cedar Key; in January 1858, the Florida state legislature officially chartered the town of Atsena Otie. By 1860, more than two hundred people lived on the island, where they established many businesses, including a pencil mill.

During the American Civil War, Atsena Otie Key suffered great hardship and significant conflict, especially when the harbor was blockaded by the Union navy's Gulf Blockade Squadron out of Key West. During this time, shipping and fishing ventures suddenly and completely stopped.

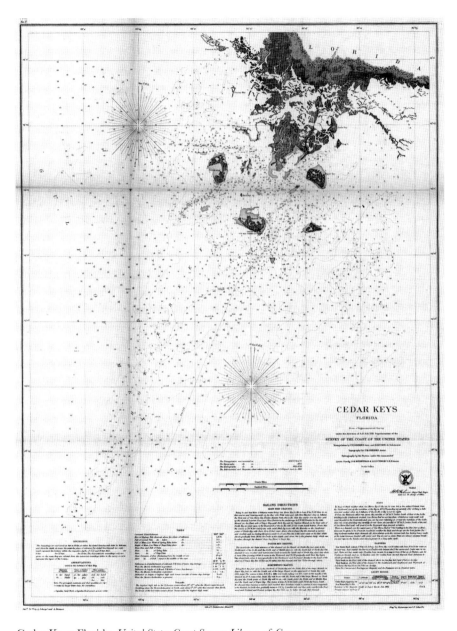

Cedar Keys, Florida. *United States Coast Survey, Library of Congress.*

Then on January 7, 1862, USS *Hatteras* landed on Cedar Key, and the U.S. Navy sailors and Marines attacked Station Number Four's rail head. The Florida State Calvary and local civilian workers did everything possible to defend the railhead and were successful initially but eventually lost their footing. The Union forces destroyed the tracks, engines and station buildings before returning to the *Hatteras*.

The navy and marines were not done with their attack on Cedar Key, and *Hatteras* boarded and sank or burned the seven blockade runners floating in the harbor at Depot Key. Then it landed, sending a small force onto the island to burn the harbor facilities.

This attack during the Civil War was small compared to other battles but was a significant event for the Union navy and has become known in history books as the Battle of Cedar Key. The battle is believed to be one of the causes of paranormal activity on Atsena Otie Key and surrounding keys due to the energy imprint the events created on the land and waterways.

Shortly after the Battle of Cedar Key, USS *Somerset* captured the *Curlew*, a blockade runner, off the island of Atsena Otie Key in June 1862. Then in the following October, *Somerset* destroyed the saltworks on James Island near Depot Key. During this attack, Union sailors destroyed more than two thousand bushels of salt and captured many civilian workers, enslaved laborers and horses.

After the Civil War, Atsena Otie Key started to boom as it recovered from the effects of war. In 1869, the Eberhard Faber Pencil Company built a lumber mill to provide wood for its pencil factory in New Jersey. The lumber mill's opening revived the island's shipping port to meet the demand for shipping timber from the mill to the factory.

This small community faced a natural disaster when a ten-foot tidal wave struck the island, washing it all away during the hurricane of 1896. Having to start anew, residents founded a new community on an island closer to the mainland. Today, Atsena Otie Key remains part of the Cedar Keys National Wildlife Refuge, approximately half a mile offshore of Cedar Key, and is only accessible by boat.

Rumor has it that a spirit rules the island and has an ancient Indian chief's curse cast on it. Some legends claim that the devastating hurricane was the curse placed on the island by a Timucuan Indian chief who was captured by white settlers along with his entire tribe and imprisoned in nearby Seahorse Key.

The chief was put to death shortly after he placed the curse on the island, claiming Mother Nature would visit with vast amounts of destruction on the island and those who imprisoned him and his tribe.

Some locals believe this curse is what continues to protect the local islands from being paved, malled and turned into a series of condominiums like the rest of the Sunshine State.

Not too long ago, in 1999, a skeleton was discovered on the island, and upon further research and testing, it was determined this skeleton was more than two thousand years old. Scientists and researchers determined the island was occupied by Native Americans at the time, followed by early sixteenth-century Spanish explorers who reached the Gulf coast of Florida. Unfortunately, these explorers brought diseases that negatively affected the Native population, resulting in vast numbers of the island's Indigenous people dying before the survivors were forced to move west onto reservations.

When visiting Atsena Otie Key, if the pesky mosquitoes and cottonmouth moccasins don't get you, you may find yourself shaking in your water shoes when facing one of the many entities that call this quiet and secluded island home.

Visitors will discover remnants of artesian wells, old structures, an old cemetery and a survey marker scattered throughout the island. These remains provide an insight into what the island was like, and the energy of the past is strong.

Besides the paranormal activity on Atsena Otie Key, nothing else happens on and around this island. It differs from what you would expect when considering a Florida tourist experience. Visiting the island is a tranquil and timeless undertaking, especially for those looking to come face-to-face with the island's spirits.

6

BALM

Hidden in the hustle and bustle of Hillsborough County is the small ghost town of Balm, an unincorporated area in Southwest Florida. Back in 1902, when the first post office was established, the city was called Doric, and twenty-four days later, it was renamed Balm.

Balm was a small farming community with a mail pick-up point on the railroad, and trains hooked mail bags as they passed through town.

The post office was built after the Seaboard Air Line Railway established a flag stop with a one-room station and water tank. The railway helped the small community boom, and by 1911 Balm was home to a blacksmith, a teacher, sawmills and a general store.

Sixteen years later, electricity arrived in Balm, and shortly after, a community telephone became available for all residents to use. By 1945, the town had more than one thousand residents living and working in the community. Families who settled in Balm were the Hicks, Sweat and Fox families, who worked, lived and died in the community. According to GhostTowns.com, Mr. and Mrs. Sweat were still living in the community at age eighty-five.[3] Mr. Sweat's father was the second postmaster, and his wife was the third postmaster for Balm, Florida.

There is little evidence Balm existed, except for a church, the original 1950 postmaster's home, a post office and a railroad station. Several visitors have reported hearing strange noises, seeing shadow figures and feeling like they are being followed when exploring what remains of Balm.

Nearby in Riverview, Florida, is the Abyss Trail at the Balm-Boyette Scrub, and many people who visit Balm go to this trail to continue their exploration adventures. Some people who have traveled along the trail experienced the feeling of acid burning their bodies, which legend claims have to do with the park and trails sitting on top of parts of an old phosphate mine. Local lore, believed by a few, claims that an ancient evil is determined to lure in victims and infect humans with the sensation of chemical burns from phosphate.[4]

Could the area be haunted by the spirits of those who perished in local phosphate mining accidents? Or is it an evil spirit or demonic entity determined to inflict pain on those who dare to visit and explore the area? There is no doubt something paranormal is happening in Balm, but the cause remains a mystery.

7

BASINGER

Basinger is a ghost town on the Kissimmee River, home to Fort Basinger, a U.S. military post, and signs of this community have vanished, except for a single historic homestead.

Legends dating back centuries include stories of the Kissimmee River being haunted, especially just north of Basinger. These legends share stories that the river is haunted by ghosts of pirates and of someone eaten by an alligator.

Dan Asfar shared a story of boating enthusiast Rick Selzer in his book *Ghost Stories of Florida*[5] about a strange encounter on the river north of Basinger. While boating, Seltzer heard some splashing around and followed an oxbow to a pond he had never encountered on previous boating trips. The water of the pond was pitch-black—blacker than black. The splashing started again, and in the center of the pond, something of significant size shot up from the water with tremendous force and fell back on the water's surface before submerging under the surface.

It was obvious that nothing physically was present above or below the surface, but the water continued churning all day. It was described as if the whole bay was alive. Seltzer immediately fled back to his campsite and, throughout the night, felt as if something had followed him back from the river.

Selzer was awakened by a moaning sound in the dead of night, so he went to investigate. Returning to his campsite, he noticed everything was destroyed and scattered, but nothing was taken. Some of his belongings

Zachary Taylor, 1850. *Library of Congress.*

were found in the trees above. He was unsure who or what did it, and on closer inspection, there were no prints or evidence of people or animals entering his campsite except his own.

So, who or what did Selzer encounter during his camping trip? Some believe it was the spirits of pirates looking for booty, and others think the moans were that of a ghost of a man who was eaten by an alligator. Seltzer could also have encountered the spirits of the army soldiers who died in the Battle of Okeechobee. The story of this battle follows:

Shortly after the Dade Massacre in 1835, the army realized it needed to push harder to "encourage" Seminoles to relocate from their homeland in Florida. It was then, in 1837, that the army called on Zachary Taylor to solve the problem previous army leaders had failed to do.

As a colonel, one of America's presidents was stationed in Basinger and marched his troops during the Battle of Okeechobee on December 25, 1837. Taylor had a presence and significant effect on the history of Florida, and his military service career led him to become brigadier general. He was ready for anything and nicknamed "Old Rough and Ready." Taylor sent many messages to his brother, claiming his time in Florida was not easy or glamorous. But it was all worth it for Taylor because his time in Florida and the thirty years he spent serving his country played a part in him becoming the twelfth president of the United States of America.[6]

The Battle of Lake Okeechobee was set among the scenery of Florida's swampland in what is known today at Bassinger. During the Battle of Okeechobee, Taylor and his troops were forced to retire at Fort Basinger after being ambushed by about 400 Seminole Indians under the guidance of chiefs Alligator, Abiaca and Billy

Hunting Indians in Florida with bloodhounds. *James S. Baillie, Library of Congress.*

Bowlegs. U.S. forces suffered 26 killed in action and 112 wounded, while the Seminoles suffered only 11 dead and 14 wounded.

After the Battle of Okeechobee, Taylor implemented a system called "The Squares Plan" to capture remaining Natives and relocate them out of Florida efficiently. However, with the interference of General Alexander Macomb, who drastically altered Taylor's agenda, all hope of completing the mission was lost. The failure of the Squares Plan resulted in a frustrated and tired Taylor being relieved from his duty in Florida.

Following his removal from duty from Florida, Taylor, with his wife, Peggy, by his side, toured the northeastern states before returning to their adopted hometown in Louisiana. A couple of years later, Taylor was elected president of the United States; he served from March 4, 1849, until his death on July 9, 1850, from cholera morbus.[7]

Fort Basinger was officially abandoned in 1850 but was reinstated for use during the Third Seminole War from 1855 to 1858. The surrounding areas remained largely settled for several years until after the Civil War.[8]

The population in Basinger fluctuated throughout the years, with pioneer families, including farmers, trappers and cattle ranchers, moving in and out of the area through the 1870s. By 1878, the town of Basinger's population had grown enough to support a general store. In 1880, a public school was built, and the population boom and the town's location along the river made it a central hub of activity, where locals shipped out crops and brought other goods on traveling steamers.

Finally, in 1893, Basinger was large enough to support its first post office, labeled "Basenger." The town's population started to decline in 1915 due to the Florida East Coast Railroad's completion because it bypassed Basinger. Soon after, in 1918, the Basinger post office closed, and in the 1920s, steamships stopped running to the town due to the new network of improved roadways.

Some spirits believed to haunt Basinger are those of Captain John Mizell Pearce. Captain Pearce died at Fort Basinger in 1897, and following his death, his wife, Martha, and son Sidney ran the ranch they lived on together. After the construction of a larger home overlooking the Kissimmee River, the property became the Pearce-Lockett Estate. In 1911, Martha died; Sidney bought the homestead from the estate, and his wife and children moved in. Later, he donated the land to the community for the Fort Basinger School to teach up to fifty local students, including his children.

When visiting the estate property, under the management of the South Florida Water Management District, people have claimed to experience strange occurrences. Paranormal activity at the Pearce-Lockett Estate includes hearing disembodied voices, extreme temperature changes, being touched and strange feelings of not being alone. It is unknown if this is Pearce, his wife or any of his family haunting the property, but many people claim to have similar experiences, and anything is possible.

Today, no remains of Basinger or old Fort Basinger exist except for the Pearce-Lockett Homestead. The homestead includes the residence, outbuildings, a barn, the schoolhouse and a family burial plot. Besides the Pearce-Lockett Homestead, the only identifying mark is a Florida State Historical Marker set on the easement of US 98 before the Kissimmee River Bridge.

8

BULOWVILLE

Bulowville is a small plantation town with few remnants of life in the 1800s. Today, the sugar mill's two-story stone walls, some stones from a mansion and a marker identifying the area of the forty slave cabins are all that remains.

Originally founded by Charles Bulow in 1821, Bulowville was inherited by his son John, who owned the plantation and sugar mill in town. Bulowville was not only a large plantation but also a village that supported the plantation's inhabitants, providing them everything needed. The city was popular for large, elegant parties, attracting famous guests worldwide, including John Audubon.

During the Second Seminole Indian War in 1835, John Bulow was a friend of the Seminoles, and it was well known that when war broke out, the St. Augustine militia planned to storm and take control of the mansion. Bulow fired several shots to warn the militia and send them away, but that did not deter the militia. They took over the estate, turning it into their headquarters and taking Bulow prisoner. Then, when the militia abandoned the mansion, they released Bulow, who felt forced to go with them. He and his slaves left all their possessions behind and relocated to St. Augustine.

John James Audubon, 1851. *Library of Congress.*

Sadly, this community was destroyed by Seminole Indians around January 11, 1836,[9] when they arrived at the mansion believing John Bulow had betrayed them. They burned down the entire town with a fierce fire that was said to have been seen more than forty miles away in St. Augustine.

After the fire, Bulow felt defeated and heartbroken by his property loss. He eventually fled to Paris, dying three years later at twenty-six.

The coquina ruins of the sugar mill, a springhouse, several wells and the mansion's crumbling foundation remain in Bulowville. The area has been engulfed by nature and reclaimed by the forest. On arriving in the former plantation town, visitors are greeted by an eerie sensation due to the reminder of the land's past, which has been marred by enslaved labor and the forceful removal of Native Americans.

Bulowville was once named one of the spookiest ghost towns in America by *Country Living* magazine,[10] and the area has been renamed Bulow Plantation Ruins Historic State Park. However, the eeriness is far more than a feeling people have when exploring this ghost town. Visitors have claimed to experience everything from being touched, hearing soft voices, seeing shadow people and feeling like an unseen force is closely watching them.

Could Charles or John Bulow haunt the land they once worked so hard to build a life on? Or are some of the 193 enslaved people who once worked the plantation haunting the ground where they were brutally treated? It could also be the spirits of Seminoles keeping an eye over the property they were once forced to leave behind.

Some visitors have shared stories about feeling uneasy because when exploring Bulowville, the air is dead silent. There are no sounds of nature, and it is almost a deafening silence.

One belief is that when the Seminoles were forced to leave the area, they cursed Bulow Plantation, and today, their spirits lurk around the park. It is common to see shadow figures and light anomalies darting around the ruins of Bulowville. It is also possible to experience unnatural cold spots, especially on hot summer days with no breezes. Some people have witnessed two tall shadowy figures emerging from the forest at the tree line and walking toward them. The two figures then disappear, vanishing into thin air before reaching them.

A local rumor claims a swamp monster lives in the forest, shaking trees, dashing through the woods and appearing quickly in one location and then another. Some believe this creature is more likely a ghost than a cryptid because of how fast it moves through the forest.

9
CEDAR KEY

Cedar Key is nestled west of Ocala on a small barrier reef along Florida's gulf coastline. This area was heavily occupied during the Civil War, and it played a vital role in attempting to prevent blockade runners from exporting cotton and lumber and importing supplies and food to the Confederacy.

The community was home to many native and migratory birds nested among the cedar trees. Today, Cedar Key acts as a federally protected sanctuary for birds, such as elusive white pelicans, roseate spoonbills and bald eagles. However, in the 1800s, the economy was supported by red cedar lumbering endeavors.

This small town met a devastating end in 1896 when a hurricane swept through the area, nearly destroying everything in its path.

Cedar Key is home to one of Florida's most famous bed-and-breakfasts—the Island Hotel. This hotel is listed on the National Register of Historic Places and was constructed in 1859 from seashell tabby with oak supports. It was first intended for the building to be a general store and post office. When the Civil War erupted, Union soldiers burned down most of Cedar Key, but luckily, the general store was left unharmed.

After the war, the Confederacy regained control of the town, and the Southern army was housed in the general store, which remained a general store with some housing accommodations. Eventually, it was transformed into a bed-and-breakfast with a small bar on the ground floor.

The construction was solid, with twelve-inch-thick walls designed to withstand countless storms and hurricanes, including the 1896 hurricane that destroyed most of the community. This hurricane severely damaged the general store, and it was transformed into the Bay Hotel, with a newly added second-floor balcony.

The hotel has experienced significant damage and major reconstruction projects over the years. It has also witnessed much death, devastation, destruction and sadness. One notable death is that of Simon Feinberg, who suspiciously died of food poisoning shortly after confronting the hotel's manager, Markham, about his illegal liquor still hidden in the attic.

During the Great Depression, the hotel was almost burned to the ground when operating as a speakeasy and a brothel. However, since most of the local fire department spent their spare time at the hotel, they were able to take swift action, saving most of the structure.

The hotel became unlivable during World War II, but then Bessie and Loyal Gibbs purchased the property in 1946, restoring it and renaming it the Island Hotel. Four years later, Hurricane Easy rampaged Cedar Key in 1950, blowing off the hotel's roof. Owner Loyal died in 1962, and Bessie retired from working at the hotel in 1973. Two years later, she died in a fire at her small cottage on Cedar Key.

After changing ownership several times, the Island Hotel remains in operation, providing locals and visitors with a place to stay and admire the long history of the property. The spirits of the hotel are just as famous as the hotel itself.

After the Great Hurricane of 1896. *Library of Congress.*

Hotel staff and visitors claim the hotel is one of the most haunted locations on Cedar Key, and at least thirteen spirits continue to occupy the historic hotel.

One hauntingly eerie story is of a small Black boy around nine who is believed to have died before the end of the Civil War. The story claims the general store manager hired this small boy to sweep up and help around the property doing routine chores. One day, the manager noticed the little boy stowing something away in his pocket and believed he was stealing something. The manager chased the boy out the back door, and he was never seen or heard from again.

About one year later, in preparation for liming, a basement water cistern was being cleaned out, and workers discovered the skeletal remains of a child. It was believed that the boy being chased by the manager climbed into the five-foot-deep, 2,500-gallon cement tank to hide from the manager. The boy was not able to climb out and drowned in the cistern.

In this basement, accessible through a single trap door at the back of the hotel, people claim to experience an eerie feeling, and the space is darker than the "inside of a black cat." In the basement, the ghost of a scared little boy hides and is often seen shivering in a corner.

Another supernatural story coming from Cedar Key is that of a Southern army private who continues to stand guard on the second floor of the Island Hotel. When the story is shared, there are missing pieces, mostly due to the fact that no one knows the entire story behind why this soldier haunts this hotel. However, the number of encounters and sightings of this apparition outnumber any other paranormal claims in Cedar Key.

It is common to encounter the soldier's spirit as the sun rises. The soldier is wearing a Confederate uniform and stands guard at attention near the doors leading to the hotel's balcony. Though dozens of guests have witnessed this apparition throughout the years, he only appears for a few seconds and then vanishes into thin air. Some passersby have seen the spirit of a Confederate soldier peering out the front windows, and it is believed to be the same watchful soldier.

Feinberg, the man believed to have been poisoned by the hotel manager, still resides at the hotel. Many have claimed to see Feinberg's spirit wandering the hotel halls at night. He likes to appear for a few moments, startling guests and staff before vanishing. No one feels threatened by his appearance, and he seems rather harmless, as long as your name isn't Markham.

There is a spirit said to haunt rooms 27 and 28 of the Island Hotel that is believed to be the spirit of a murdered prostitute. This spirit is thought to be a prostitute from when the hotel was a brothel and speakeasy during Prohibition, and she is very friendly. Many guests feel her presence sitting on their bed in the middle of the night and her gentle kiss on the cheek before bed. She slowly disappears into a smoky haze at the foot of the bed when spotted.

Former owner Bessie Gibbs is believed to be hanging around her former home and hotel operation. Bessie is said to be behind the mysterious movement of hotel items, including rearranging furniture, moving pictures and closing doors. She is commonly blamed for locking guests out of their rooms, and she is seen walking around rooms and through the walls in the middle of the night. When the apparition is described, it greatly resembles Bessie, who was known to play jokes and be playful. She appears to continue to interact with guests as she did when she was alive.

Bessie is also known to relax on the second-floor porch swing, one of her favorite places to sit when she maintained a proprietary interest in the hotel.

After a séance was held in the hotel with the hopes of conjuring up the spirit of Bessie, it resulted in an unscientific conclusion that her upstairs sleeping room, now guest room 29, is haunted by several spirits. Additionally, a psychic investigation concluded at least thirteen ghosts in the hotel haunt the rooms along with Bessie. Many guests have heard footsteps behind them in the halls, and when they turn around, no one is there.

Several visitors have also claimed to encounter the spirits of two Native American Indians, an unidentified tall, slender man, a moonshiner and a fisherman. The hotel's front porch is another paranormal hot spot, where people have witnessed lights flickering, doors opening and closing, cold spots, breezes and mysterious drafts.

Some researchers believe Bessie's room acts as a portal to another dimension, a way for entities from other worlds to visit Cedar Key.

Though the hotel is one of the focal points for paranormal researchers, the entire community of Cedar Key is filled with stories of spirits, apparitions, shadow figures, cryptids and more. Some have referred to Cedar Key as a sleep town, filled with dark trails, boarded-up buildings and mossy grasslands, perfect for the setting of a Stephen King story.

10

CHOKOLOSKEE

The general store and trading post opened by Ted Smallwood in Chokoloskee in 1906 now serves the community as a museum and time capsule. Sharing the dramatic details of Florida's pioneer age, the Smallwood Trading Post is home to many spirits refusing to leave their beloved community.

There is an urban legend about the notorious outlaw Edgar Watson that says he was killed in the area and haunts Chokoloskee today. Watson was known to have a bad temper and was responsible for many deaths, including the murder of sugarcane field workers, so he wouldn't have to pay them.

The legend claims the spirits of his victims followed him around town, refusing to let him rest. The spirits succeeded in tormenting Watson, helping him turn over a new leaf when a woman was allegedly killed at Watson's Chokoloskee home in 1910. Wanting to redeem himself, he sought to avenge her death by tracking down and killing the man responsible.

While tracking the murderer, Watson stopped by the Smallwood Trading Post to purchase ammunition. In the general store, he bragged about his plans to kill a murderer. His ranting and raving brought the attention of the locals, who had had enough of his behavior and were fuming mad about his need to kill every person he disagreed with.

The angry locals banded together and took matters into their own hands, and an angry mob in the trading post gunned down Watson. Legend claims he has never left the trading post, and since he never managed to avenge the woman's death, he is punished to exist forever in his version of hell.

The spirit of Watson appears before visitors exploring Chokoloskee; he has a chest full of gunshot wounds, and his face is frozen in a twisted eternal scream.

Because Watson could not avenge the woman's death, local gossip shared stories about the spirit of this woman who followed him to the Smallwood Trading Post. Because her death was never avenged, she cannot rest and, along with Watson, eternally roams in and around the trading post. The spirit of the woman is spotted more often than that of Watson.

There is also a female spirit barely recognizable as a human, almost as if it has been rotted to the bone. This gruesome apparition is often spotted in front of a mirror, combing her remaining hair and crying. One visitor saw her reflection in the mirror behind him and believed he was about to be confronted by a real-life zombie. However, when he turned around, no one was there.

It is unknown what this spirit truly is. Some beliefs include she is a zombie, a deformed ghost or a wraith. Some researchers believe this decaying spirit is the same as the murdered woman's, but no one has been able to provide evidence connecting the two apparitions.

Other reports of paranormal activity at Smallwood's Trading Post are in Ted Smallwood's bedroom, where he would occasionally spend the night when expecting late-night shipments. Many people have claimed to see a woman in the dresser mirror as they walked by it on the way to the restroom. Shadow figures have been seen pacing and moving through the bedroom at all hours of the day.

The building and museum owners are often contacted by local residents reporting hearing trespassers in the store late at night. Upon their arrival, there is no one there and no evidence anyone has broken into the structure.

ELDORA

Eldora is an uninhabited area in Volusia County set within the Canaveral National Seashore. This desolate area is south of Bethune Beach and west of County Road A1A at an elevation of only three feet above sea level.

Eldora was a booming community at one point, relying on profits from the local orange groves in the latter part of the nineteenth century. Unfortunately, most of the crops were destroyed by a freeze, resulting in many residents fleeing, leaving the community nearly completely abandoned. The last remaining resident, Doris "Doc" Leeper, died in 2000. Eldora never regained its lost population and is one of the state's most infamous ghost towns with no permanent "living" residents.

Today, Eldora is home to two marine research facilities shared by Daytona State College and the University of Central Florida. This ghost town is also home to many mysterious entities and spirits of those who once loved living in this citrus-filled community.

Visitors exploring Eldora can enjoy peaceful walks through the century-old live oaks and return to a thriving village or stand where sportfishermen once stood fishing in Mosquito Lagoon Aquatic Preserve waters. The last remaining structure in town is the Eldora State House, home to the town's post office, school, hotel and town hall. The State House was placed on the National Register of Historic Places in 2001.

Many visitors claim to feel an eerie presence, but most relate those feelings to hearing whispers of the town's past. No documented evidence indicates Eldora is haunted, but many researchers have seen shadow figures, darting light anomalies and strange nonhuman sounds from the lagoon.

12

ESPANOLA

Central Flagler and southern St. Johns Counties conceal a secret within their scrub forest. Hidden among the dense vegetation is a red-brick ghostly highway running for ten miles that was once a popular route for tourists in "Tin Can Trailers" and Model-T Fords driving from as far away as Chicago. These tourists traveling Old Dixie Highway wanted to experience the exotic and tropical wilderness available only in Florida.

Back in 1880, the community of Espanola was home to three families: the Hunters, Helms and Raulersons.[11] Several descendants from these families continue to live in Espanola.

Today, a few segments of the brick highway are part of the Old Brick Road, built in 1915, offering visitors a rugged and bumpy trip down memory lane. Time has not been favorable for this brick highway; it contains many potholes, and several portions are buried in the sand.

Before the Old Dixie Highway became obsolete in 1926, Espanola was located along the highway and was a welcoming site for weary travelers. The community was home to a rest stop, hotel, restaurant, post office and barbershop after the construction of the railroad in the region and the completion of US Highway 1 and State Highway 11, running from Bunnell to Flagler. Many of the bricks from the highway were pulled up and used to build the Bunnell Elementary School gymnasium. Several residents in the area also received bricks from the highway to build fireplaces, patios, driveways, sidewalks and various paving projects.

Visiting Espanola is truly an Old Florida experience, and today the quiet settlement remains with a few structures still standing. When visiting this area, explorers often find they are alone most of the time. There may be one or two cars that pass while driving the brick highway, but other than that, it is relatively quiet. It is more common to see a black bear, snake, hawk, bald eagle or armadillo than to see another human being.

There is a sign along the highway going into Espanola that says, "Proceed at your own risk." The sign is more likely a safety warning pertaining to the driving conditions, but one cannot help but wonder if there is a hidden ghostly meaning to the sign.

The area is so desolate, it is eerie and scary to explore during the day. One visitor was exploring Espanola with his wife, and they were calling for their dog when then suddenly, they started hearing another voice calling for the dog around the corner of the old dirt path. Later, he heard someone calling his name, and the voice started laughing.

Upon looking at photographs captured during their adventures in Espanola, the couple caught what appears to look like a woman's shoulder wearing a dress in one of their pictures.

When darkness falls on Espanola, many brave visitors experience strange voices coming from the wooded areas and see a basketball-sized ball of light float through the trees. There are also many reports of shadow figures walking along paths and darting among the trees along the red-brick highway.

13

FORT DADE

Egmont Key was named in 1763[12] in honor of the second Earl of Egmont—John Perceval—an Irish House of Commons member. Throughout its history, the islands in this area have had everything from Spanish conquistadors to nuclear submarines pass by their shores as they enter Tampa Bay.

Egmont Key has witnessed many military movements and occupations, including serving as a U.S. military outpost with a lighthouse. During the Third Seminole War, it served as a temporary internment camp for Seminoles before relocating out of Florida. Then, Union troops retained control of the islands, using the lighthouse as a watchtower during the Civil War to target Confederate blockade runners and place a chokehold on the South's economy.

During the Civil War, depending on who had control of the island, fort and lighthouse, Egmont Key and the area around Fort Dade housed Confederate prisoners, Union sympathizers and escaped slaves. In 1864, a cemetery was established for interning thirteen Union and Confederate soldiers from 1864 to 1865. The community continued to use the cemetery until 1909, when the bodies within the cemetery were removed to national cemeteries in other areas of Florida and Georgia.

Key West was devastated by yellow fever, which quickly spread through the island community in November 1882. Egmont Key and Fort Dade were used as U.S. Marine Hospital Service stations for those infected with yellow fever.

Fort Dade was constructed during the Spanish American War on Egmont Key Island off the shores of Tampa Bay. War conflict and the threat it presented Florida's southwest coastline inspired the fort's construction to provide communities with formidable defenses.

After the war, a small town developed around Fort Desoto, and between 1899 and 1916, more than seventy buildings were constructed. The community was home to NCO quarters, a fire station, a gymnasium, a movie theater, a bowling alley, tennis courts, shops and more. The town was home to about three hundred residents, with brick streets winding between the wood-frame buildings.

In April 1917, the United States joined World War I, and Fort Dade was being used as a center for National Guard Coastal Artillery Units, and the island's population nearly doubled. In 1919, a power plant was constructed, and this was the last major structure built on the island. By 1920, many residents no longer occupied the island, and the population dropped to below three hundred, with most residents working as a skeletal crew for the Coast Artillery.

October 1921 brought devastation to Fort Dade when a hurricane rampaged through the area, damaging many areas of the fort and destroying the boathouse and wharf. The hurricane's destruction was the final event that led to the decision to close the fort, placing it under "caretaker" status in May 1923.

After shutting down the fort, the military used the island for target and tactical practice. Then between 1935 and 1936, four fires raged across the island, and to prevent future fires, the Coast Guard received permission to level many remaining structures that were deemed fire hazards. In addition to the fires, the island was also affected by several hurricanes that came through the area during the same time, further damaging the fort's and town's remains.

During World War II, Egmont Key saw military activity resume in the area by serving as a harbor entrance patrol station and being utilized as an ammunition storage facility. The War Department worked to clear roads, refurbish structures and build new structures when it took control of the island.

In 1939, the Coast Guard started managing and operating the lighthouse on Egmont Key, leaving the keeper's residents vacant. Soon after taking over lighthouse operations, the two-story keeper's home was demolished to build a one-story barracks. Today, the only inhabitants of the island are its caretakers.

After years of being the background for military operations, Egmont Key became a national wildlife refuge in 1974 and is now managed by the U.S. Fish and Wildlife Service. The area was also named to the National Register of Historic Places in 1978. In cooperation with the U.S. Fish and Wildlife Service, Florida established Egmont Key State Park in 1989.

Unfortunately, years of exposure to fire, wind, ocean tides, rain, vandalism, Mother Nature and neglect have taken a toll on the fort's structure. The ruins of Fort Dade remain on the northwest shore of Egmont Key but are crumbling and deteriorating from the Gulf Coast community's heat, humidity and weather conditions. Since the foliage has taken over the island, some parts of the fort's structure are unrecognizable, and several ruins from Fort Dade are partially or fully underwater.

The fort has various tunnels and underground compartments formerly used to store gunpowder and shells. Though all military supplies have been removed, these areas are dark and damp; some say many soldiers remain behind.

There is one story about a group of college students who wandered up on the beach of Egmont Key and discovered the ruins. Upon exploring, laughing and having fun in the summer sun, something happened that scared the girls from wanting to go into the underground areas. The guys, acting brave and macho, picked on the girls, but they encountered something in these areas and never made it inside. No one knows what happened to scare and prevent them from entering. The stories only share that they did not continue entering the darkness and returned to the beach.

Author Greg Jenkins shared several ghostly accounts happening in and around Fort Dade in his book *Florida's Ghostly Legends and Haunted Folklore: The Gulf Coast and Pensacola*. One story is from a park ranger who reported seeing the spirit of a man dressed as a Civil War soldier while patrolling on Egmont Key. Several others have reported seeing shadowy figures lurking around the lighthouse, and some have spotted a pale face peeking out from one of the lighthouse windows.

Several former park rangers have reported hearing phantom gunfire ringing through the fort.

So what could be causing paranormal activity around the island and within the ruins of Fort Dade? Several experts speculate it could be the spirits of Seminole warriors, Spanish explorers, Union and Confederate soldiers and former lighthouse keepers and their families.

14

FORT DESOTO

Fort DeSoto is set on the southwest tip of the island and was used to house a class of armament consisting of twelve-inch mortars to be fired simultaneously in an artillery battery. It was the perfect location because it was hidden from enemy ships. After all, they were buried in dense vegetation and sand. The fort never saw combat; however, it remained a significant part of modern weaponry history and served as a sub-post of Fort Dade on nearby Egmont Key.

The area surrounding Fort DeSoto was occupied for centuries by the Tocobaga Indians from 1000 to 1500, who lived on Mullet Key. The site was visited in 1513 by Juan Ponce de León, whose ship was anchored off the island to have barnacles scraped from the vessel. Ponce de León's expedition was attacked by Timucuan Indians, resulting in one soldier's death, the first European battle casualty in North America. The attack on Ponce de León's expedition was also the first documented use of artillery in the Tampa Bay area.

Other Spanish explorers who landed on Florida's west coast included Pánfilo de Narváez in 1528 (between St. Petersburg Beach and Clearwater) and Hernando de Soto in 1539. De Soto landed on the southern portion of Tampa Bay. Despite numerous Native American attacks, the fort's namesake explored more than four thousand miles of shoreline with ten ships and seven hundred men as he tried to claim Florida as part of Spanish colonization.

Future Confederate general Robert E. Lee surveyed the area as part of a detachment of U.S. Army Engineers in 1849. It was recommended

Mullet Key and Egmont Key become the site of fortifications to help with the coastal defense of Florida. Though the U.S. government did not build forts on the islands, Union army troops were stationed on the islands during the Civil War to aid in naval blockades of the Tampa Bay area.

In 1882, these keys were used for military reservations during the Spanish American War; however, no fortifications were built. Mullet Key was named Fort DeSoto in 1900 as part of the main operation and housed batteries of artillery and mortars ready to use to protect Tampa Bay against invading forces. The fort was completed in 1906 using a foundation created by a mixture

Juan Ponce de Leon. *Library of Congress.*

of seashells, stone and concrete. When completed, this post included a large barracks, mess hall, administration building, guardhouse, blacksmith shop, carpenter shop and hospital. The area also has several brick roads, concrete sidewalks and a narrow-gauge railroad used to move materials, supplies and various items around the post.

The fort was deactivated in 1922, and in September 1938, Pinellas County purchased the areas on and around Mullet Key to create a public-use site. Shortly after the purchase, the county commissioners leased the land and two buildings on the extreme southern side of the property to Percy L. Roberts. Roberts used the area to operate a boat service company using the *Hobo* (a passenger boat) to the island, offering fresh fish dinners and allowing guests to rent fishing tackle. His vision was to create a venue, including a hotel and restaurant, on the island, perfect for sightseeing, group outings, fishing and dining on fried mullet.

Using one of the buildings, Roberts created a place where visitors would enjoy a meal, prop up their feet at the end of a long day, enjoy a cool beverage and relax along the Gulf waters. This structure became known as Mullet Key Lodge.

The lease agreement between Roberts and the Pinellas County Commissioners was short-lived. The U.S. War Department needed the island as a bombing range for the U.S. Army Air Corps. To meet the need, the county commissioners had to rescind the lease agreement, ending Roberts's profitable business, and sell the land to the government.

After World War II, the U.S. Army Air Forces (formerly the U.S. Army Air Corps) no longer needed Mullet Key and sold the land back to Pinellas County, along with the adjacent keys—Sister, Hospital, Rattlesnake and Scratch. Mullet Key and Fort DeSoto were designated as a county recreational area, opening it up to the public.

Throughout the years, Florida's sweltering climate, unrelenting mosquitoes and harsh living conditions were only a few causes of the many tragedies near Fort DeSoto. The isolation and living conditions at Fort DeSoto caused many enlisted men to avoid reenlistment, and several died from heat stroke and suicide. Sergeant Charles L. Scott died by suicide at the age of twenty-seven in 1902 and was buried in the Fort Dade Post Cemetery.

Additionally, several service members experienced near-death events from weapons misfiring and accidental mortar fire issues. Injured soldiers were transported off the island and reported to have died from their injuries several days later.

Fort DeSoto Beach was also used as a makeshift morgue when a Coast Guard buoy tender, the *Blackthorn*, and a ten-thousand-ton oil tanker, the *Capricorn*, collided. The collision occurred on January 28, 1980, about three-quarters of a mile west of the Sunshine Key Bridge, and killed twenty-three Coast Guardsmen. One of the dead crew members from the *Blackthorn* was found floating in the water near Mullet Key. The collision was documented as the worst peacetime disaster in the U.S. Coast Guard's history.

On May 9, 1980, a severe storm caused the *Summit Venture*, a thirty-four-thousand-ton carrier, to ram into the Sunshine Skyway Bridge.[13] The accident collapsed 1,400 feet of the roadway, sending a Greyhound bus, three cars and a pickup truck into the waters below.

Mullet Key was used as a base of operations as rescue workers recovered the thirty-five bodies, including a six-month-old child who died. During the recovery, two unidentified victims washed ashore at Fort DeSoto Park. The bodies of other victims were placed in plastic bags and transported by motorboat to Fort DeSoto Park.

This accident was called one of the worst bridge disasters in U.S. history, and many other victims suffered extensive impact injuries. The flag was flown at half-mast at the emergency headquarters at Fort DeSoto Park.

The list of deaths in and around Fort DeSoto is long; the two aforementioned incidents are the most notable and tragic of all accidents in the area. Throughout the island's history, there have been many other tragic deaths with unknown causes. Could these deaths, tragedies and incidents be what is causing much of the paranormal activity in the area? Some believe the spirits of the victims from the bridge and Coast Guard accidents roam the area looking for answers about the cause of their untimely death.

The following deaths, accidents and incidents throughout Fort DeSoto's history may also be causing some mysterious events to occur in the area.

The first soldier to die on Mullet Key was Calvin B. Eastman, who died during his military duties against the Seminole Indians.

According to naval documents, Daniel "Scott" Whitehurst and his first cousin John Alexander Whitehurst were shot by Confederate sympathizers. Scott was buried on the shores of Mullet Key in an unmarked grave. John paddled away by boat toward Tampa Bay and was found by a Union sympathizer who took him back to a refugee encampment on Egmont Key. John died the following day and was buried on the island until all burials were moved to the National Cemetery in St. Augustine.

In 1965, a man was found dead in an apparent suicide in the water near Fort DeSoto Park. Another man who died from an apparent self-inflicted gunshot wound was discovered in 1981 at Fort DeSoto Park.

A unique feature of Fort DeSoto Park is the series of burial mounds where three massive whales, dolphins, sea turtles and manatees have been interred.

Additionally, the nearby Sunshine Sky Bridge is the site of an estimated 236 suicides since it opened in 1987. The number of suicides and deaths at the bridge makes it one of the deadliest bridges in the United States.

In relation to the Sunshine Skyway Bridge, many have reported seeing people walking to the edge and jumping from the bridge, only to disappear before entering the water below.

Some have also reported seeing a female apparition hitchhiking. When she is picked up, drivers notice she is nervous, wanting drivers to move to the other lane. Eventually, this spirit vanishes from the vehicle.

A ghost bus has been seen traveling near those on the fishing pier, which is where the original bridge was located. Witnesses claim to feel a breeze and smell gasoline when the bus passes. On closer inspection, an older woman is seen waving and grinning in the bus's rear. Then, the bus plunges downward through the bridge.

At Fort DeSoto, many who have stayed past the sun setting have heard hushed voices echoing off the walls of the southernmost bunker. Phantom footsteps can also be heard when sitting quietly in the bunker. Some people have witnessed an apparition of a dripping wet, fully clothed man appearing at the fort, leaving behind wet footprints. Some have reported a similar occurrence, but it was of a wet soldier who pulled himself out of the ocean waters, walking through the fort as he drips water everywhere.

Phantom footsteps can also be heard in the fort's small powder room, and many feel uneasy when in this area of the fort alone.

Mullet Key was once used as a quarantine area for those infected with yellow fever. The ghost of a woman quarantined during this time went insane when hearing the news her children had all died from yellow fever. Some people claim to hear a woman's voice cry out and see the apparition of a woman searching for her children on the island.

The ghost of a man searches for his lost lover along the shores of Fort DeSoto Park and is seen wearing a blue shirt. After pacing along the shoreline, he is seen walking into the water and disappearing.

The Fort DeSoto Park toll plaza is also where many people have spotted the ghost of the "Friendly Trout Fisherman." He has been seen wading in the water near the grass flats. This spirit is fond of women, often coming out of the water to interact with them and disappearing shortly after the conversation begins.

Other theories about who might be haunting Fort DeSoto Park and the surrounding areas include members of the Tocobaga tribe who were killed by Spanish explorers and the diseases they brought to America. Some believe the spirits of Spanish explorers, including Hernando de Soto, roam the campground at night.

Today, Fort DeSoto is part of the Fort DeSoto State Park, which is managed and operated by Pinellas County and is part of a series of offshore keys—Madelaine Key, St. Jean Key, St. Christopher Key, Bonne Fortune Key and Mullet Key (the main island). The group of islands is accessible by a toll road from the mainland and a causeway. Remnants of the old fort, buildings and a museum are available for exploring throughout the state park.

Camping is available at Fort DeSoto Park, and though the campground feels quiet, it is home to many spirits haunting the area. When the sun goes down, it is quite possible to encounter at least one of the spirits, including those of soldiers, that haunts the location. Overnight campers have reported hearing gunshots and voices.

15

FORT DRUM

Found west of the Florida Turnpike is a small ghost town used to house a fort during the Second Seminole War. Fort Drum was initially a fort, but soon after its construction, residents started moving to the area, especially after the Civil War. Those looking for jobs in the cattle industry settled in the surrounding area.

In 1842, after the end of the Second Seminole War, the U.S. Army started to build a network of forts across Central Florida, with military roads connecting them. Where the roads from Fort Bassinger to Fort Vinton (north of present-day Vero Beach) and from Fort Kissimmee to Fort Jupiter intersect is where Fort Drum was built.

Like many other forts in Florida, it was only used by the U.S. Army briefly and then left abandoned. However, the surrounding community grew slowly because the land was the perfect place to raise cattle.

Today, Fort Drum contains the remains of the town's cemetery and an antique and collectibles store housed in the original Fort Drum School. The town's cemetery is set in the middle of the city, covering almost eight acres. Many of the area's first settlers were buried in the cemetery, and some believe their spirits still roam the area.

Many visitors have experienced various unexplainable events. When exploring Fort Drum, it is common to hear phantom noises and come face to face with playful spirits.

The LeRay Historic District is the backdrop for an urban legend about the spirit that continues to haunt the LeRay Mansion in Fort Drum. Reports of paranormal activity within the mansion include doors opening and closing and the toilet flushing independently. Some estate visitors have had their clothing tugged when no one else is around them.

Other paranormal accounts at this location include the lights suddenly turned off with a loud popping noise. Then when someone says, "Knock it off!" the lights immediately turn back on. Unsure it was paranormal or faulty electricity, they called in an electrician, but he wouldn't go into the basement alone because he had his own ghostly experience.

16

FORT JEFFERSON

One of Florida's most fascinating ghost towns is Fort Jefferson, located within the Dry Tortugas National Park about seventy miles west of Key West.

Fort Jefferson was the ideal location for the United States military to establish an advanced post. The fort secured the spacious harbor, making it possible for the military to monitor ships patrolling and entering the Gulf of Mexico and the Straits of Florida.

The Dry Tortugas, where the fort is set, offered ships a harbor making it possible for them to take a break from the waters and resupply and refit. The harbor also provided ships and their crews a refuge when severe storms churned the waters. The location of the Dry Tortugas was perfect because it was nestled along one of the world's busiest shipping lanes, making it a great military asset.

Fort Jefferson was one of the largest forts ever built in America, and despite its failed completion, it was a vital part of protecting Florida's western coastline. The fort was crucial in a chain of coastal forts stretching from Maine to California.[14] These forts symbolized that the United States wanted to be left alone, and Fort Jefferson fulfilled its intended role and was never attacked. The fort stood to protect the peace and prosperity of a young nation.

Upon its construction, it was deemed that the existing Garden Key lighthouse and its keeper's home were included within the fort's walls. The lighthouse continued to guide ships through the Dry Tortugas and

Top: Fort Jefferson, Garden Key, Key West, Monroe County, Florida. *Historic American Buildings Survey, Library of Congress.*

Middle and bottom: Fort Jefferson, large detached magazine, Garden Key, Key West, Monroe County, Florida. *Historic American Buildings Survey, Library of Congress.*

was eventually replaced with a metal tower set on top of the adjacent wall in 1876.

During the Civil War, Fort Jefferson was under federal control, housing several hundred prisoners of war. However, it was later discovered that most prisoners housed at this fort were deserters and robbers and not actual POWs.

Special civilian prisoners arrived at the fort in July 1865. These prisoners, Dr. Samuel Mudd, Samuel Arnold, Edmund Spangler and Michael O'Laughlen, were all convicted in the conspiracy of the assassination of President Abraham Lincoln. Dr. Mudd was sentenced because he was the one who helped set John Wilkes Booth's leg after he broke it jumping onto the stage at the Ford Theater after shooting President Lincoln.

Two years later, in 1867, Fort Jefferson was affected by a yellow fever epidemic, which quickly spread throughout the fort. The epidemic provided an opportunity for Dr. Mudd to assist the sick; however, despite his attempt to help, many prisoners died from yellow fever, including fellow conspirator O'Laughlen. Dr. Mudd's efforts to help treat the sick did not go unnoticed. President Andrew Johnson eventually pardoned and released Dr. Mudd from prison at Fort Jefferson.

After the army abandoned Fort Jefferson in 1874, it was used as a coaling station for warships and was where USS *Maine* stopped during its

Top: Abraham Lincoln. *Library of Congress.*

Bottom: Fort Jefferson, large detached magazine, Garden Key, Key West, Monroe County, Florida. *Historic American Buildings Survey, Library of Congress..*

Fort Jefferson, large detached magazine, Garden Key, Key West, Monroe County, Florida. *Historic American Buildings Survey, Library of Congress.*

1898 historic sailing from the Tortugas to Havana, Cuba. The fort was used during both world wars before it was no longer needed as the "Guardian of the Gulf."

At this point, the War Department turned the fort over to the Marine Hospital Service to serve as a quarantine station. However, due to damage from hurricanes and vandals, Fort Jefferson quickly deteriorated.

In 1902, the Navy Department received ownership of the property and added coal rigs and water distilling plants. When the 1906 hurricane destroyed these structures, the navy left the fort abandoned again until two years later, when it was set aside as a federal bird sanctuary.

Built in the nineteenth century, Fort Jefferson was never completed and has been abandoned, leaving a magical fort open for visitors to explore dungeon-like alcoves, dark rooms and legendary spirits. Several structural renovations and historic preservation projects have been completed, making visiting and enjoying the Dry Tortugas and Fort Jefferson possible.

The fort is a paranormal researcher's dream because it has a history of executions, murder, epidemics and more. Many people who visit the island fort return home with a chilling story to share with friends and family.

The hallways throughout the fort have an eerie feeling, and some experience an unusual energy that makes them nauseated. Several people have spotted apparitions and shadow figures walking through the halls and hiding in corners of the fort's interior.

Those who brave the island overnight camping on the shores of Fort Jefferson have reported seeing strange lights and hearing devilish sounds coming from within the fort's walls. Once the sun sets, the spirits come alive at the fort, and it is possible to experience paranormal activity.

17

FORT KING

The long history associated with Fort King began in 1827 when it was constructed to act as a garrison to protect Seminole Indian lands from new people moving through the area and provide a way to maintain the peace. The land was used as a buffer and a means to enforce policies set by the Seminole Indian Agency. A shift in beliefs and attitudes and a lack of funding prompted this garrison to close. The fort was named for Colonel William King, who commanded the Fourth Infantry.

Not long after the closing of the garrison, President Andrew Jackson ordered the Seminoles to leave Florida and start moving into Oklahoma. That was when Wiley Thompson was brought to Florida, replacing a kinder, gentler Indian agent. The concept of an "Indian agent" created chaos and turned the fort area into a powder keg waiting to blow.

At this point, the Seminoles refused to move, claiming those who signed the Treaty of Payne's Landing were not approved to speak or act for the tribe. Their refusal caused tensions to grow, and in late December 1835, troops were sent from Fort Brooks near Tampa to reinforce those serving at Fort King. However, these reinforcements led by Major Francis Dade never arrived at Fort King because they were ambushed in what has been named the Dade Massacre.

On the same day as the Dade Massacre, an outspoken Seminole attacked Thompson at Fort King. Wiley Thompson was shot fourteen times and scalped. Four other men from the fort were taken into custody by the Seminoles. When the Second Seminole War ended, the tribe came through the area, burning all buildings down to the ground. However, the locals were strong, and the area was rebuilt one year later until it was abandoned in 1843. Those leaving the fort area took what was left of the fort and used the materials to build new homes, businesses and the Ocala courthouse.

One legend shares the story of two lovers—a young private and a Seminole woman. He approached her despite the tensions between their people during the Seminole Wars. While blood was spilling from both sides of the war, the two found love at a time when their relationship was considered forbidden.

Andrew Jackson, *Library of Congress.*

The two lovers met in secret late at night and made plans to move far away once his service time was over. Before they could live happily ever after, far from the devastation of war, he was called away deep into the Ocala woods for a scouting trip. The Seminoles ambushed him and the others in his scouting group, and all were believed to have been killed.

When the Seminole woman (or as some legends call her, a maiden) received word about the ambush, she returned to the spring where they used to meet to grieve her lost love. However, her soldier survived the attack and returned to Fort King, immediately visiting the spring behind the fort. There he found her body floating face down in the spring waters. Heartbroken, he took out his sidearm and shot himself in the head. He believed if they could not be together in life, they would be together on the other side.

There are many reports of paranormal activity near the springs of Fort King connected to this legend. Some people encounter an unusual fog that follows the path of the spring on some nights, especially during the months of December and January, when these deaths are believed to have occurred. Some visitors have reported seeing a couple walking along the waterway and sometimes wading through the water. The couple is often described as being transparent and having a blue or white glow to them. As the couple gets closer to each other, they tend to disappear, never really being able to touch.

Other paranormal occurrences near the spring include light anomalies, a phantom gunshot and unexplained cold breezes on hot summer nights. This inexplicable activity is believed to be related to the two lovers and connected to the Seminoles' anger about Fort King and its occupants. There are also some reports of something much darker lurking in the shadows of the fort.

Locals report unexplained lights hovering in the sky, floating near the ground, and mysterious shadow figures peeking from behind trees and the fort's structure. Many believe some of the paranormal activity is far beyond ghosts remaining behind haunting the fort. Some feel the land may be cursed, especially since some nearby businesses have trouble staying open, and there is a high suicide rate within a couple-block radius of the fort.

The Seminoles could have placed a curse on the land, upset they were being forced out of their homes. Though there is no evidence or documentation, some urban legends claim that Indian burial mounds were found throughout the area, which could have been Native American burial sites. These mounds, if they truly existed, were dug up and disturbed during the construction of Fort King and nearby structures.

Many driving by Fort King see mysterious lights floating over the lawn near the front of the park. This area was where the cemetery used to be before the bodies were relocated to the cemetery in St. Augustine. This area of the fort is known to be the most active, aside from the springs.

Some people have seen soldiers walking their dogs through the area at night. The soldiers start to approach and then disappear as they get closer. These soldiers were also spotted by a man driving by during the day; he saw two men dressed in uniforms carrying guns. He thought they were part of a reenactment and pulled his vehicle over to talk to them. As they approached them, they faded away.

When visitors see spectral soldiers during the daytime and talk to the park rangers about any special reenactments or events, they are told nothing special is planned. Then visitors are advised, "Don't worry, this happens all the time" or something similar when they share their story with the park ranger.

A lot of ghostly activity is occurring in and around the visitor's center of Fort King—reports of knocking at the door and no one there, strange voices and violent smashing sounds.

Today, visitors cannot see the original Fort King, but they can explore a re-creation of the fort that was constructed to showcase its importance in Florida history. Even though the original structure no longer stands, there is no shortage of paranormal activity at Fort King.

18

FORT PICKENS

Fort Pickens is set on Santa Rosa Island within the Gulf Islands National Seashore as one of four military forts constructed to protect Pensacola in the 1800s.[15] This fort is accessible by foot and boat, offering many opportunities to experience something unexplainable.

This historic military fort has a pentagonal shape and was named after Revolutionary War hero Andrew Pickens. Completed in 1834, it was one of few Southern forts that remained in Union control during the Civil War. Fort Pickens remained in use until 1947 and is now managed by the National Park Service.

When the United States decided to fortify all major ports after the War of 1812, it hired French engineer Simon Bernard, to design Fort Pickens. Construction lasted from 1829 to 1834, using 21.5 million bricks and labor provided by enslaved persons.

On January 20, 1858, Fort Pickens fell victim to a major fire when USCS *Robert J. Walker* was at the fort. Several boats and USCS *Robert J. Walker* worked together to fight the fire. The ship's captain received communication from Army Corps of Engineers captain John Newton acknowledging the ship's role in saving the fort.

When the first shots of the American Civil War were fired, Fort Pickens had been left vacant since the conclusion of the Mexican-American War. Despite its battered and rickety condition, Lieutenant Adam J. Slemmer, who was in charge of the U.S. forces at Fort Barrancas, felt Fort Pickens was the most defensible post in the Pensacola area.

Upon making this decision, Lieutenant Slemmer abandoned his position at Fort Barracas to relocate to Fort Pickens. When Florida declared its secession from the Union on January 10, 1861, Slemmer destroyed over twenty thousand pounds of gunpowder at Fort McRee and then moved his small force of fifty-one soldiers and thirty sailors to Fort Pickens.

Slemmer refused to surrender to the demands of Colonel Henry Chase of the Florida militia and defended the fort against threats of attack until he was relieved by Colonel Harvey Brown and USS *Brooklyn*.

Confederate forces attacked Fort Pickens on October 9, 1861, during the Battle of Santa Rosa Island but were defeated and forced to retreat with ninety casualties.

General Andrew Pickens. *Library of Congress.*

While tensions between Confederate and Union forces grew, the Northern troops worked to shell the Confederate forts nearby—Fort McRee and Fort Barrancas. On November 22, 1861, Union warships—*Niagara* and *Richmond*—sailed into the bay to begin bombarding Confederate strongholds. This attack lasted two days, and Fort McRee was nearly destroyed along with the town of Warrington and the navy yard.

To finish off Confederate forces in Pensacola, the Union launched a second bombardment on New Year's Day 1862. Again, Fort McRee was nearly destroyed, and many buildings near Fort Barrancas were burned. Feeling defeated and running low on supplies, Confederate troops started doubting their chances of winning the Battle of Pensacola. Finally, on May 10, 1862, the last Confederates in Pensacola surrendered to troops at Fort Pickens.

Fort Pickens was turned into batteries for the army in the late 1890s and early twentieth century to be used by the Endicott Board. This board was a group headed by Secretary of War William C. Endicott that changed military batteries to be spread out over a

Lieutenant Adam Slemmer. *Library of Congress.*

Fort Pickens: Pensacola Harbor, Florida. *Currier & Ives, Library of Congress.*

wide area, concealed by concrete parapets keeping everything flush with the surrounding terrain. Battery Pensacola was housed at Fort Pickens, and obsolete weapons were repurposed during World War I.

The U.S. Navy was interested in Fort Pickens during World War II. It strengthened its defenses to strategically use the fortifications against the threat of German U-boats already in operation in the Gulf of Mexico.

All of the activities, devastation and threats of war have imprinted high levels of energy at Fort Pickens, and many souls continue to occupy the fort well into their journey through the afterlife. Everything from apparitions of Confederate soldiers and Native Americans to demanding and conversational voices can be seen and heard throughout the fort. Several paranormal investigators and visitors have captured the words "Get out of here!" as an EVP, and some have claimed to have heard it while in the jail area as if someone was standing behind them, giving them a warning.

Several apparitions have been reported wandering the tunnels, halls, cells and grounds of Fort Pickens. One person reported seeing the ghost of a man wearing a long black trench coat and hat, similar to other sightings of the Hat Man. Others have seen a Confederate soldier approach them with a heavy smell of cologne and then lead them toward the cannon storage area.

Several people report seeing the spirit of multiple Confederate soldiers who died in battle, and some have captured strange mist and ghostly images behind bars in the jail in their photographs. Some photographs show light anomalies resembling swirling portals in the jail cell area.

It is also possible for the spirits of Native Americans, including Apache Chief Geronimo and his braves, who were held prisoner at Fort Pickens. Geronimo and his braves were imprisoned at Fort Pickens from October

1886 through May 1887, while their families were sent to Fort Marion in St. Augustine. It is believed these are the spirits that have been heard and seen roaming the fort. Reports of hearing voices speaking in a Native American tongue have been heard and captured as EVPs out on the fort lawn.

It is common to hear phantom cannons firing, smell gunpowder and blood, get touched on the shoulder or hear moaning as the jail cell doors open and close. Some have felt like someone was breathing on their neck when no one was behind them, and many have heard a man's voice kindly saying "Hello."

When exploring Fort Pickens, there is a heavy emotional feeling; some have felt their chest tighten as they approach the jail cells.

There is something paranormal happening at Fort Pickens. It is almost as if someone is trying to get the attention of the living, and they are succeeding.

19

GAMBLE PLANTATION

South of Tampa has many historic buildings and communities full of early American history. Ellenton, Florida, is one of these communities at near-ghost town or working ghost town status and is home to the historically haunted Gamble Mansion and Plantation.

Major Robert Gamble Jr., the son of a wealthy tobacco grower from Tallahassee and war hero, arrived in Manatee County in 1843, when he took advantage of a new federal program—Armed Occupation Act of 1843. Under the new act, he was awarded 160 acres of land for free under the agreement he would clear the land and cultivate it. His land was available after the Second Seminole War ended, and local Native Americans were removed from the Florida Territory.

He continued to work the land, eventually securing a land patent in 1847, allowing him to purchase an additional 3,300 acres for $10,000. Six years passed before Gamble finished building his home and plantation on the property because the land required extensive work cleaning and draining a network of canals.

His new home was two stories, constructed from red brick, with two-foot-thick walls and eighteen large pillars standing twenty-five feet tall and eighteen inches in diameter supporting the roof and upper and lower verandas. The pillars and construction methods crafted a home resembling the appearance of Greek Revival–style architecture. Though the home felt massive, by southern plantation standards, the Gamble Mansion and Plantation was relatively small, with only ten rooms.

When completed, the property had a wharf set on the Manatee River for shipping and receiving goods.

Though Gamble used enslaved labor to run the plantation and produce tens of thousands of pounds of sugar, it was not enough to keep him out of debt. After everything from poor market conditions, overuse of debt and multiple hurricanes, he was forced to sell the plantation for $190,000 in 1859 to John C. Coefield and Robert Davis from New Orleans. The slaves were individually listed in the sale of the property, and when the sale was completed, most of the slaves were transported and relocated to New Orleans.

Sadly, none of the slave quarters remain today, but at one point, according to the 1860 census, the property had fifty-seven slave houses on the plantation housing 190 slaves. It is believed that Coefield owned most of the 253 slaves living in Manatee County; however, very little documentation is available beyond general census data.

This page: Gamble Mansion. *Historic American Buildings Survey, Library of Congress*

When the Civil War erupted, Manatee County was set along the edge of untamed wilderness, and Florida was sparsely populated with only two major cities—St. Augustine and Key West. When Florida seceded from the United States, it mostly offered the Confederacy beef cattle, sugar and salt instead of providing newly enlisted service members. The Cowboy Cavalry drove cattle north to supply Confederate troops, and Jacob Summerlin, the King of Crackers, actively helped with this mission by driving an estimated twenty-five thousand beef cattle to the front lines between 1861 and 1863.

The soldiers of the Ninety-Ninth U.S. Colored Infantry first destroyed the gristmill in Manatee before crossing the river toward the sugar mill at Gamble Plantation, which was under Confederate control. Soldiers loaded the mill with artillery shells, igniting them to create an explosion heard and felt across the river in Manatee City.

The impending end of the Civil War resulted in the evacuation of the Confederate capital, Richmond, Virginia, forcing Secretary of State Judah P. Benjamin to flee. Declaring, "I'll never be taken alive," Benjamin used the name M.M. Bonfals, a Frenchman, as he proceeded to Florida on horseback to avoid capture. Upon his arrival, he spent several months at the Gamble Plantation.[16]

During his stay, a Union patrol arrived at the plantation, and he began his final journey to safety to Bimini in the Bahamas, which he reached on July 10, 1865. A few months later, he made his way to Southampton, England.

The Judah P. Benjamin Chapter of the Daughters of the Confederacy purchased the mansion and sixteen acres of the plantation in 1925. Though it was left vacant for many years, the State of Florida finally took over the property after it was donated to the state, helping restore it and maintaining the Gamble Plantation as a reminder of Florida's role in the Civil War.

The park, operated by the state, includes the Gamble Plantation and Mansion and a restored wood-frame, two-story Victorian-style home built in 1872 for owner George Patten. The grounds also house the Confederate Veterans Memorial Monument, erected on October 10, 1937, and the forty-thousand-gallon cistern used to supply the home with fresh water.

At the plantation system's peak during the Civil War, Florida was home to approximately four hundred operational plantations with enslaved labor, and today, the Gamble Mansion is the only surviving antebellum plantation in the state.

As the only remaining antebellum plantation mansion still standing in South Florida, the Gamble Plantation and Mansion is likely haunted by pre–Civil War spirits, former slaves, slaveholders, Confederate soldiers and more. These spirits could be looking for a familiar location or suffering a punishment for the painful past this area contains.

Those who were enslaved at the Gamble Plantation lived a life with immense hardships, but it was their sense of family and the close-knit community that gave them hope. As on many other plantations in the South, enslaved people developed a unique culture with various spiritual practices and oral storytelling traditions. It is believed that some of the enslaved peoples from the Gamble Plantation gathered in the afterlife to continue with their storytelling traditions.

Paranormal activity throughout the Gamble Plantation's property includes hearing strange noises, seeing shadow figures lurking among the trees and sensing a heavy presence in the mansion and several areas throughout the plantation.

Secretary of the Navy Judah P. Benjamin, Confederate States of America. *Library of Congress.*

Hearing an eerie melody is another interesting occurrence experienced in the area surrounding the Manatee River. It is believed this melody is residual energy caused by an incident dating back to the Seminole Wars. During the Battle of Braden Castle, pioneers were under attack by Seminole Chief Billy Bowlegs, famous for razing villages in the late 1800s.

During this attack, one of his tribal members was shot and captured. When the pioneers were helping bandage the Native's wounds, they learned of a famous legend from the area.

The legend shared by the captured Native American was about a Calusa princess, the Timucuan chief's son and their forbidden love affair. The two lovers would secretly meet along the Manatee River, somewhere between the Gamble Mansion and the I-75 bridge.

The two gathered at the site where a mysterious musical sound emanated from the river. This sound could be heard on certain moons and has been part of many poems, local legends and lore.

Today, the sound can be heard during the months of April and May at Rocky Bluff. The source of the sound is still a mystery, and some have seen the apparitions of two people in Native American attire appearing during these months as the music starts to fill the air.

20

GULF CITY

G ulf City was a small village nestled on the banks of the Little Manatee River at Tampa Bay. Unfortunately, time, hurricanes and vandals have made Gulf City nearly disappear. So when seeking out remnants of this quiet village, you will most likely encounter only the spirits of those who once lived in the area.

Though almost every sign of Gulf City's existence has vanished, there are many unique stories related to the paranormal encounters happening throughout the area.

One of the most unique paranormal stories is related to sightings of prehistoric animals that roamed the area known as Gulf City more than 1.5 million years ago. A local paleontologist, Frank Garcia, discovered more than thirty thousand bones in 1983 at the Leisey Shell Pit. The bones were those of prehistoric animals, such as saber-tooth cats, giant sloths, llamas and more. A historical marker was installed to identify the discovery spot, which is now hidden underwater.

Locals have reported hearing strange growling sounds in the distance and seeing what is believed to be a large animal out of the corner of their eye, and when they turn around, there is nothing there.

More than one million years later, Gulf City was the home to Native inhabitants who settled along the shores of the Little Manatee River. The small villages were discovered by archaeologists in the early twentieth century near the mouth of the river. The dig site revealed human remains and hundreds of artifacts giving insight into the lives of the people who called this area home for thousands of years.

Hernando de Soto invaded the area south of Gulf City and documented the first historical account of these Natives. When he and his men marched north through the site, they encountered an abandoned village where the Little Hillsboro River meets the bay. Unfortunately, as troops moved through the area and progress required roads to be constructed, many of the mounds left by the Uzita were destroyed.

It is believed that not only the spirits of de Soto's men haunt the area but also many Uzita spirits remain behind to watch over the land.

Many locations throughout Florida, including near the Gulf of Mexico, are haunted by legendary pirates. Pirates known to be in the Gulf City area and believed to remain behind include the Pious Pirate, Ben Margoza; Henry Ross; and more.

Gulf City was officially founded in the mid-seventeenth century by British pirate Margoza. Though the town's residents tried to make it successful, its location and lack of industry started its decline in the nineteenth century. In 1865, the city had seventy-six residents and a post office, but by the 1920s, the town had been completely abandoned.

Since it is challenging to get to Gulf City, there are not a lot of reports about paranormal activity, but those who remember going to the town or who live nearby believe it is haunted by many who once roamed, lived and tried to thrive in the area.

21

HAGUE

Hague is another small town in Florida that boomed in the 1800s as a railroad community but recently has been forgotten and left for the spirits to regain control. Like many towns during this era, Hague developed due to the railroad industry in Florida, allowing goods to be transported in and out of town. The Savannah, Florida and Western Railway was newly completed in early 1884, connecting High Springs and Gainesville.

The railroad helped export large quantities of fruit and vegetables to northern states, which continued into the twentieth century.

This small town was home to about seventy-five residents, including early settler and landowner Archelaus Hague. The wealthy landowner eventually became a postmaster.

During its prime, the town had several cotton mills, sawmills, three stores, two lumber mills and three churches. As the community continued to grow, a post office and an express office were later constructed and added to the many businesses in Hague.

Unfortunately, the incursion of the boll weevil forced many mills in Hague and other small towns in Florida to collapse. Only a handful of residents remain, and this town reportedly has more spirits roaming the streets than living.

Those who have chosen to make Hague their home have said that the spirits of the former settlers are still with them. The most common report of paranormal activity in Hague is hearing disembodied voices, especially where the cotton mills once stood.

Though many residents would not consider Hague a ghost town, compared to the population in the late 1800s, this community does qualify. Many structures stand as a reminder to the small village of what life was once like in Hague. Remnants of the old railroad station, water tank and the restored old School House–Methodist Church remain standing.

22
CAMP HELEN STATE PARK

Paranormal researchers looking to explore a quiet, peaceful destination in northern Florida will want to check out Camp Helen State Park. Set on U.S. Highway 98 along the western edge of Panama City Beach, this 183-acre park tells historical stories to those wanting to explore, and those willing to listen can hear the stories of the dead being shared in the cool Gulf of Mexico breezes.

The peacefulness of the park and the stunning beaches make it impossible to imagine such a beautiful place as a ghost town. Yet it is a ghost town with ghostly residents. It is rumored the park is home to not one, not two, but three spectral residents that roam the state park grounds.

The land where the state park stands today was purchased in 1928 by Robert E. Hicks for a summer retreat for his family. The Alabama company Avondale Textile Mills later bought it, and the land was renamed Camp Helen. Avondale Textile Mills wanted to use the area as a resort destination for vacationing employees. Many historic buildings, including the lodge, remain standing today, with many recently undergoing major renovations and restorations.

During the ghost walks hosted by the Friends of Camp Helen State Park from 2006 to 2013, rangers and guests experienced some unexplainable incidents, which left them leaving the state park with spooky ghost stories to share with those willing to sit and listen.

One spirit believed to be haunting Camp Helen State Park is that of a young enslaved girl named Rose, who was killed by Indians in 1843. Rose was a passenger on a ship caught in a New Year's Eve storm, forcing the ship to run aground near the area. The vessel required repairs, and those on the ship made contact with local Indians, who were first believed to be friendly. However, while the captain was searching for food, the Indians attacked and Rose was killed. She was buried in a shallow grave, and when the moon shines on the beach, she is often spotted walking along the waterline.

Some people have reported seeing a female entity matching the description of Rose walking in the moonlight along the water. When they get closer, she is gone and there are no footprints or disturbances in the sand.

Some visitors have also claimed to hear the scream of a woman believed to be Rose, but that could easily be explained as a natural occurrence. The area of Camp Helen State Park houses a large population of panthers, and when they howl in the distance, it can sound like a woman's scream.

The only grandson of Margaret Hicks is believed to be another ghost haunting Camp Helen State Park. Legend claims the little boy wandered away from his nanny, headed to the waters of Lake Powell and drowned. On the day of his death, he was left in the care of Hicks's cook and nursemaid while Hicks went to Panama City for a grocery run. The little boy, George, is called Gigi by many who work and visit the park.

He happily played in the courtyard garden while the cook and maid prepared lunch. When they called him for lunch, he didn't respond, and they couldn't find him anywhere in or around the garden. Tragically, the little boy wandered to the boat dock in front of the family's lodge and fell into the water.

The first documented appearance of Gigi was in 1996 when a passing fisherman spotted a little boy playing on the beach. Though that is not typically an unusual sight, the caretaker told the fisherman that nobody lived on the property and no little boys were living in the immediate area.

Sightings of Gigi continue, and many see him walking along the water and standing or sitting on the old pier. Some visitors have also reported hearing what sounds like a young boy walking around and playing upstairs in the cabin.

Another spirit spoke to a guest visiting the former Hicks family lodge. Hugh Comer of Avondale Textile Mills, a prim and proper Sunday school teacher from Birmingham, was a guest at the former Hicks family lodge. He was invited down to check the place out, and during his stay, he resided in Margaret Hicks's old room.

During his stay, at night, he was woken up by the ghost of Captain Phillips. The legend claims the namesake of the nearby Phillips Inlet loomed over

Comer in the darkness and, in a deep voice, declared, "This is my house; get out of my house!"

Others who have encountered the spirit of Captain Phillips have also claimed he told them to get out. They also feel this spirit has a mean and menacing presence, often making people uncomfortable and forcing them to leave the building.

It is safe to say that Camp Helen State Park has many permanent residents who do not want to leave the area. It seems as if the locals and those working the park have become comfortable knowing these spirits remain behind, haunting the area.

23

HOLOPAW

The Creek Indian word Holopaw means "walkway" or "pavement," and the community was a stop along the Kissimmee Valley extension of the Florida East Coast Railway. The town is so small it is often missed when driving through the area.

So what is this small town in Central Florida that is easily missed, especially if you blink too long? Though Holopaw may be small by today's standards, it was once a booming railroad town where the sawmill employed hundreds of locals.

The Florida East Coast Railway made its presence known in Holopaw between 1911 and 1929 when it constructed a building in the community to use as a stop along the line. It was advertised that this was the second complete mainline to Miami, also known as the Kissimmee Valley Branch.

J.M. Griffin opened the sawmill in Holopaw in 1923, selecting a location to construct the building near the railroad. The sawmill was the largest operation in the St. Cloud area and featured one of the first all-electric sawmills in the United States. To house the hundreds of employees, the town slowly built up with residents of all sizes, followed by businesses, such as a town store, saloons, restaurants and more.

During the Great Depression, the sawmill opened by Griffin closed, and the new mill owner, Peavy-Wilson Lumber Co., took over operations in 1935. Under new ownership and management, the mill hired over one thousand workers to handle timber, turpentine and sawmill operations. During this time, the town's population peaked at more than two thousand.

The town continued to flourish, attracting new residents looking for jobs at the sawmill, until one day in 1947, the railroad line traveling through Holopaw was discontinued. Shortly after, the mill closed and the town soon collapsed. Many residents left town to seek employment elsewhere, and the local post office was officially shut down in 1954.

Today when traveling through Holopaw, there is an eerie feeling associated with the few remaining homes, abandoned buildings, vegetation overgrowth and tree limbs scattered on the ground.

Legend claims those brave enough to explore Holopaw come face-to-face with phantom limbs littering the ground's surface. Upon witnesses getting closer to inspect the arms or legs, they vanish. It is theorized that these phantom limbs belong to former sawmill employees who lost them in workplace accidents.

Other paranormal claims include seeing shadow figures moving through the brush and among distant treelines.

For those who dare to venture out and explore, Holopaw will not have much to see, but there is a greater chance of encountering a spirit than a living, breathing human being.

24

HOPEWELL

A small plantation, the Turner Plantation, was built in the area of Hillsborough County before the Civil War. The town that developed around this plantation was originally called Callsville. George W. Wells established the post office on May 14, 1883, to serve the two hundred residents living in Callsville. The Hopewell Baptist Church was built by early residents in 1870 and was named after Hopewell, Alabama.

Set among citrus groves, the plantation was the start of a booming community with many businesses and residents, leading to the development of Hopewell. Though Hopewell was a thriving community in the late 1800s and early 1900s, very little is known about why the town is now abandoned.

Not much of Hopewell has been left standing today. Exploring the area will reveal the remains of the McDonald House, Hopewell Baptist Church, the Hull House, a cemetery and various cracker-style homes. Though these structures remain, the area is mostly citrus groves and other vegetation.

Several residents claim that when walking through the groves around dusk, they can hear voices believed to belong to residents who once called Hopewell their home. The voices have been described as deafening at times, and some refer to the sounds of a choir of voices calling out to the living.

25

HOWEY-IN-THE-HILLS

Set in Central Florida is a small town that was once a booming community home to the first citrus juice plant in Florida. Howey-in-the-Hills has a population of less than two thousand, making it a working ghost town with a unique past.

The town was named after the man who founded the city and built the juice plant—William John Howey—and the rolling hills that surrounded the city. He made his living buying acres of land, planting orange groves on the properties and then reselling them to inventors. Howey lived a lavish lifestyle and built a mansion, Howey Mansion, which stands abandoned.

The Howey Mansion is a beautiful Mediterranean Revival home he built in 1925, and it has been the community's crown jewel for many years.

When the Volstead Act passed, enforcing Prohibition under the Eighteenth Amendment in 1919, the Howeys installed a hidden basement. This basement was designed to stash their alcohol secretly.

Howey hosted many parties and welcomed many dignitaries and the rich and famous, including President Calvin Coolidge.

Aerial view of juice and packing plant, Howey-in-the-Hills, Florida. *State Archives of Florida, Florida Memory.*

During the Great Depression, Howey turned to politics and continued to be an active politician until he died in 1938. His widow, Mary Grace Hastings, remained in the mansion for another forty years after his death. Howey, his wife and their children, William and Lois, are interred in the family's mausoleum in the backyard of the mansion's property.

Today, the Howey Mansion is a mesmerizing haunted mansion key to unlocking much of Howey-in-the-Hills' history. The mansion's 8,832 square feet include twenty rooms on 3.63 acres and is home to various spirits and paranormal activity.

Everyone who passes or enters the mansion's property reports an overall eerie feeling. Visitors have felt they are being followed when no one is

Top: Close-up view showing entrance to the historic Howey Mansion. *State Archives of Florida, Florida Memory.*

Middle: Close-up view of the gateway to the historic Howey Mansion. *State Archives of Florida, Florida Memory.*

Bottom: Bird's-eye view overlooking fountain in courtyard at the historic Howey Mansion in Howey-in-the-Hills. *State Archives of Florida, Florida Memory.*

behind them. Several have reported being touched by an unseen force and spotting various shadow figures from the corner of the eye. Upon further investigation, there is no one else in the area.

So is the Howey Mansion haunted? Many visitors claim it is not, but there are some reports of various unexplained phenomena occurring, which leads others to believe there is a great possibility the abandoned mansion is home to many former residents and possibly the Howeys.

26

INDIAN KEY

In the 1830s, Indian Key was known for its lucrative salvage operations and was the first county seat for Miami-Dade County. However, pirating and raids affected the island, forcing the inhabitants to flee and abandon it.

Nothing remains behind on the original Island Key except for a few foundations and labeled streets. Besides that, much of the abandoned island is overrun with vegetation and is only accessible by boat.

Though the island is abandoned, the presence of the former residents can still be felt among the ruins of this ghost town.

Florida legend claims the ghost of Jacob Housman continues to live in Indian Key, haunting those who dare to venture to the island. Several people have reported encountering a spirit believed to be Housman's and have experienced strange activity, which could be associated with his spirit.

Housman is the former owner of Indian Key, which he purchased in 1831 to build his wrecking empire. During this time, wrecking and salvaging cargo from shipwrecks was legal and an extremely lucrative endeavor. His kingdom included a hotel, dwellings, a store, cisterns, wharves and warehouses.

Housman constantly feuded with other salvagers and developed a reputation for shady business practices. He was behind the decision by the legislative council to make Indian Key the county seat for Miami-Dade County in 1836.

The island fell under attack by Native Americans on August 7, 1840, who attacked the well-stocked store and many structures. During the attack, Dr. Henry Perrine was among the at least six people who died during the raid,[17] which is believed to be associated with the difficulties during the Second Seminole War. Other inhabitants of Indian Key, including Housman, managed to escape, and they fled the island.

Housman later died in a wrecking accident, and it is rumored his wife buried his body on the island. The grave has been vandalized but has been replaced with a replica.

Upon the others fleeing, the U.S. Navy took control of the Indian Key for the Second Seminole War. A couple of years after the end of the Second Seminole War, the Dade County seat was relocated to Miami in 1844. After the war, the upper keys, including Indian Key, were returned to the government of Monroe County.

In 1856, the U.S. Army remained behind, stationing a few members on Island Key to help protect the two remaining families from the threat of attack during the Third Seminole War. The island was also used as a hospital for the navy and as a staging area for the construction of sailing vessels and the construction equipment for the Carysfort Lighthouse and Alligator Reef Lighthouse.

Other paranormal accounts happening at Indian Key include phantom cannon fire, gunshots, ritual drumming, screams and feeling like there is a heavy presence in the air. Several people have reported hearing footsteps and the crunching of vegetation beneath feet from behind them while walking and exploring the island, only to turn around and see they are alone.

27

KENANSVILLE

K enansville is about sixty miles southeast of the Greater Orlando urban region and is a small, unincorporated community in Osceola County. The community was founded in the late 1800s as one of the many Central Florida areas to experience a boom associated with the Florida East Coast Railroad. The town was named in 1914 after Henry Flagler's third wife, Mary Lily Kenan.

During its boom, Kenansville's main export was cattle transported by the railways. The town's location also made it convenient for travelers to stop for a rest and locals started offering services, including restaurants and lodging, to accommodate the needs of weary travelers.

Though the railway did run through the town, today, there are no remnants of the railroad because the tracks and depot are gone. Only a few buildings remain, including the Old Schoolhouse and the Heartbreak Hotel.

An interesting legend claims that Elvis Presley once stayed in the Heartbreak Hotel in Kenansville. Presley's experiences at the hotel inspired him to write his song "Heartbreak Hotel." No reliable sources prove this, but several online publications reference the legend.[18] Some claim it is more likely the hotel's owner loved the tune so much that he renamed it after the song.

It is rumored the old schoolhouse in Kenansville is haunted, and several people have claimed to have seen two glowing eyes coming from the school's top left window. On foggy days it is common to see shadowy figures walking through the thick fog and then vanishing. For those patient enough to hang around the schoolhouse, it might be possible to hear the playful screams of children playing in the yard.

28

KERR CITY

K erry City is a spooky ghost town in Florida set on Lake Kerr in what is now the Ocala National Forest. This small town was originally founded in 1884 as the second settlement in Marion County. When exploring the city during the day, it seems like a typical abandoned town; everything is peaceful and quiet. However, when the sun sets and darkness fall on the city, it turns into a scene right out of a horror movie.

The nighttime scenery may be enough to send a person's mind into thinking spirits surrounding them—especially when the antique windows rattle in the wind and the floorboards cry out with creaking sounds as you walk through the 130-year-old structures. However, there is no illusion here. Those who walk through Kerr City will be surrounded by many spirits and come face-to-face with something unexplainable.

Eventually, after growing to one hundred residents, Kerr City showed signs of a fully functioning town. A post office, general store, sawmill, school/church and three-story hotel were constructed in the city to meet the needs of the residents and those visiting. The town was the perfect destination for those traveling from the St. Johns River to Ocala.

View of the site for the new town: Kerr City, Florida, circa 1885. *State Archives of Florida, Florida Memory.*

Unfortunately, the town's orange groves suffered from freezing temperatures in 1894 and 1895, destroying the town's main economic resource. The following year, Kerr City was deserted. The town suffered another unfortunate event in 1907 when the beautiful hotel, the Lake Kerr House, burned to the ground. Luckily, the fire did not spread through the town, and several of the buildings in the Kerr City Historic District survived and remain standing today.

One paranormal story shared involves a couple visiting Kerr City and realizing it was closed, so they decided to hike around the area looking for a place to camp. After fighting off hungry mosquitoes, they quickly realized they were not alone on their adventure. When the couple came upon a dead end, the girlfriend, who was experiencing a creepy feeling, wanted to turn around; however, the boyfriend insisted on continuing, searching for a path to follow.

Finally, the couple reached a clearing and encountered something they could only explain as straight out of their nightmares. They came across a small cemetery with about twenty graves arraigned in neat columns with small headstones. The headstones were old, and the names were no longer legible.

The sight of the cemetery was not the most frightening thing they encountered during their hiking adventure. When the couple turned to leave and return to where they came from, they noticed dark shadows rising from the ground. The couple stood there as the shadows slowly moved closer and the air became thick and heavy.

The thick air made breathing challenging, and the couple started coughing, choking and feeling like smoke was filling their nostrils. Then, suddenly, they were saved by the reliable midday summer rain. When the rain started, the shadows disappeared and the couple realized they were no longer in the cemetery but were back by where they met the dead end in the hiking path, and the sun shone.

Could the spirits of those in Kerr City have created an illusion to keep the couple from reaching the town? Or were the shadows the victims of what some legends claim to be associated with a natural disaster long before Kerr City became a town?

Nothing is on record about a natural disaster in the area, but those who believe the urban legend think it could have been a fire or a flood. The legend claiming it was a fire shares stories about a group of people who went camping in the forest one night and the forest caught fire. Everyone in the camping party died and was buried in the small cemetery, which has been avoided ever since.

For generations, folks have whispered, sharing stories that the old wooden houses in Kerr City are haunted. Reports of strange sounds were heard within the walls of the old houses. Some people have reported seeing apparitions, chills and feelings of otherworldly presences looming over them as they visit the town.

Ghostly figures have been spotted walking up and down the stairs of buildings, including the town's two-story post office. Some believe the apparition in the post office is of the former postmistress, Sarah, who continues to live upstairs. Many have seen Sarah, who is recognizable by her bright-red hair, walking the stairs or pacing on the structure's top floor. It is also believed a second ghost has joined Sarah at the post office. Some believe the spirit is a woman named Alice, seen in the building and looking out windows.

Hotels in Kerr City. Lake Kerr. *State Archives of Florida, Florida Memory.*

Another legend in Kerry City is that of a young woman, Grace, who died at nineteen and is buried in the town's cemetery. Some believe she might still be looking for her family, and her apparition is often spotted roaming the streets in town. Those looking for her grave will easily find it, as it is encircled with a rusty, ornately decorated iron fence.

Only one person remains behind caring for Kerr City, which is not available to the public to explore, visit or investigate any remaining buildings. He is the great-grandson of the town's founder and owns the entire village, including the fourteen structures, among them the oldest Texaco station in Florida.

As the second-oldest platted town in Marion County, Florida, there is no doubt that many spirits have remained behind to haunt Kerr City.

29

KORESHAN STATE PARK

ESTERO, FLORIDA

Chicago doctor Cyrus R. Teed developed a new religion, Koreshanity, in 1869 after changing his name to Koresh. Teed was a distant relative of Joseph Smith, the founder of Mormonism and the Latter-day Saint movement. After Teed's revelation that he was the new Messiah, he changed his name to Koresh, the Hebrew form of Cyrus.

He placed himself as the head of the religion and developed a devout following. Teed and his followers wanted to re-create the Garden of Eden, which would have been challenging, if not impossible, to achieve in Chicago. In 1894, Teed and his followers relocated to Florida to build a commune—the Koreshan Unity. This area in Florida was to be their New Jerusalem.

To help prove their beliefs, including one of their core beliefs that the Earth was one large hollow sphere, Koreshans used education, science and art as a significant part of their community. They also built and operated a printing facility, cement works, boat works, sawmill, store, bakery and hostelry.

It was a unique theory about the earth and was explained through stories claiming the hollow orb contained continents and oceans within and the sun, moon and stars were only reflections of the core's ball of gas.

The theory that the Earth was a hollow orb made it around the world and was one theory that intrigued Adolf Hitler. Hitler believed that by building something powerful enough, a telescope, he could watch over the White House and see what President Franklin Delano Roosevelt was doing.

Koresh's more than two hundred followers were so dedicated and believed their Messiah would rise from the grave that in 1908 they held onto his body, waiting for him to resurrect. Three weeks later, the health department had to step in and force them to dispose of Teed's body. His followers placed his body in a mausoleum on the beach, which many years later was washed out to sea during a hurricane.

After Teed's death, his following slowly declined, and the last of his followers died in 1982.

Today, the Koreshan State Park is home to historic buildings and gardens created by Teed and his followers as a testament to their unique beliefs and lives as Florida pioneers. The park is set on the banks of the Estero River, secluded under towering oaks, making it the perfect place for spirits to hide in the shadows.

It is believed that the spirit of Teed and many of his followers haunt the Koreshan State Park and its museum. Several believe the spirits of the doctor's followers hang around the area awaiting the resurrection of their leader, who died more than one hundred years ago. Some theorize that the Koreshans remain behind in the afterlife to watch over the commune and protect the land.

Top, middle: Aerial view looking north over the Koreshan State Historic Site park in Estero, Florida. *State Archives of Florida, Florida Memory.*

Bottom: A few Koreshans by the gate in front of the Koreshan Unity's Guiding Star Publishing House in Estero, Florida. *State Archives of Florida, Florida Memory.*

Several witnesses have reported seeing shadow people walking along the trails, disappearing, disembodied voices coming from the buildings and seeing floating light anomalies.

Some visitors have captured an image of a female figure through the window of one of the buildings. Upon further analysis of the image, they concluded that no one was standing outside the structure close to the window to throw off a reflection, and they confirmed the building was locked and no one was inside.

One person reported that when hiking in the area with a friend, they encountered a hellhound, which they believed followed them for three days. According to mythology, a hellhound is a creature responsible for guarding or serving hell, the devil and the underworld. Not much information is available about this encounter except for a random comment on an online post about the Koreshan State Park.

Teed's failed attempt at achieving utopia is forever preserved at the Koreshan State Historic Site, one of Florida's most unusual and intriguing ghost towns.

Top: Close-up view of historical marker at the Koreshan State Historic Site park in Estero, Florida. *State Archives of Florida, Florida Memory.*

Bottom: Dr. Cyrus, R. Teed. *State Archives of Florida, Florida Memory.*

30
LAWTEY

Lawtey was a small town founded in 1877 by thirty Chicagoans who named the city after the son-in-law of one of the new residents. At its peak, the city had a booming economy and was home to many mansions, a cotton gin, a sawmill and schools. The agriculture industry was the most successful asset those living in Lawtey had.

By 1885, the town was home to approximately 250 people who worked and survived by growing and harvesting oranges and strawberries. The town's agricultural industry and economy declined significantly during the Great Depression, which led many residents to leave to avoid the wealthy northerners settling in the area.

During the early 1900s, Lawtey fell victim to a violent element and residents were left scrambling when one of the many shooting events occurred in town. Residents rarely left their dwellings after dark; when they did, they were often accompanied by their reliable guns. Rival gangs vied for power during this time, and murder was not uncommon.

The violence and struggles of the Great Depression made it impossible for Lawtey and its residents to recover.

Civil War reenactors participating in various events in Lawtey claim to occasionally capture light anomalies in photographs, which many believe are the spirits of soldiers interacting during the reenactments. An increase in paranormal activity during reenactments could occur for many reasons, including the spirits not realizing the war is over or because they want to participate in something familiar to them.

Other paranormal experiences at Lawtey include feeling bone-chilling breezes on hot summer afternoons and shadowy figures rustling throughout the woods.

Lawtey is a ghost town or a semi-ghost town, and chances are more spirits are roaming the city than the living.

31

MICANOPY

The small town of Micanopy has deep historical roots and has been nicknamed the "Town that Time Forgot." Visiting the city takes travelers back to what the community was like in the mid- to late 1800s. Micanopy is a historical community in Florida that has withstood the test of time.

Town records indicate Micanopy began as a Timucua Indian village in the 1500s, and Hernando de Soto visited the area. As the oldest inland town in Florida, Micanopy was included in a land grant in 1817 created by the king of Spain.

The Second Seminole War in December 1835 caused massive devastation to the town of Micanopy. The city had to be evacuated during the Battle of Micanopy, and many of the town's buildings were burned and destroyed. After the war, residents returned, rebuilt the city and made it an agricultural center for the state.

The Herlong Mansion, built in 1845, is now a bed-and-breakfast but was home to Inez Herlong, who is believed to haunt the building.

The town is a little over one square mile and is nestled between Gainesville and Ocala, Florida. The streets of Micanopy offer visitors a charming atmosphere away

Florida Southern Railway depot, Micanopy, Florida. *State Archives of Florida, Florida Memory.*

Cholokka Boulevard, looking south on the business square, Micanopy, Florida. *State Archives of Florida, Florida Memory.*

from city life. Several surviving homes have been renovated and preserved, creating a unique tribute to the town's historic past.

Micanopy allows visitors to return in time and provides a wonderful environment for spirits to thrive.

Paranormal investigators have reported a child spirit at the Herlong Mansion that plays with RemPods and Boo Bears, causing the alarms and lights of these devices to go off. In the upstairs bedroom of the mansion, researchers have recorded high spikes of electromagnetic fields, cold spots and unexplained noises.

Local legends believe that Inez still haunts the mansion and has been spotted looking out her bedroom window. Witnesses have claimed that the doorknob rattles all night when one of the upstairs bedroom doors gets locked. But if left unlocked, nothing happens.

Inez is believed to haunt the mansion grounds and has been spotted wearing a long blue dress with sleeves to her wrists. This apparition has brown hair with gray highlights piled high on her head. She stands below bedroom windows staring up, and when spotted, she slowly fades away. It is not certain this is the spirit of Inez, but many believe it is.

There is one legend about a maid at the Herlong Mansion who was washing in a tub, and when stepping out, she slipped and started to fall. An unseen force stopped her from falling, pushing her back to standing.

Other paranormal activities in the mansion include doors opening and closing and sounds of footsteps walking on the floor above when no one else is in the home. Smoky figures have been spotted floating up the stairs and vanishing at the top.

Close-up view of the Herlong Mansion at 402 N.E. Cholokka Boulevard in the Micanopy Historic District. *State Archives of Florida, Florida Memory.*

Several guests staying at the bed-and-breakfast have been woken up in the middle of the night by a fine mist of water sprayed on their faces. It is common to hear a woman's voice softly speaking and smell perfume. Some have witnessed a woman in white appear in mirrors and then disappear when they turn around.

Could the woman speak and the perfume be the famous woman in white who has been spotted roaming the grounds of the Herlong Mansion? Could this be the same apparition many believe to be Inez? It is still uncertain who or what is haunting the Herlong Mansion, but many visitors and researchers believe something or someone is haunting it.

32

PICTURE CITY

Imagine the perfect life with pristine streets, magical landscapes and Hollywood-ready homes. The ideal Hollywood community is exactly what a company, Olympia, wanted to develop in the 1920s when it created a small Grecian-style town that would be used to create epic movie sets. Plans for the town continued for many years during the land boom, and when that boom collapsed in 1926, construction and planning for Picture City ended.

Olympia was bankrupt, and its dream of building the perfect Hollywood town was abandoned along with the city. Then, nearly two years later, Olympia was almost completely destroyed by a hurricane.

Various roads, some unfinished, others destroyed, head to Olympia from Hobe Sound. These roads lead the way to what planners envisioned would be a Hollywood-like movie studio in Florida. The community was believed to thrive, with more than forty thousand residents strolling the streets, visiting parks and enjoying the seaside paradise. One of the brains behind the project was Maurice Fatio, a famous architect known for designing many luxurious mansions on the Palm Beaches.

Unfortunately, the city did not become what it was meant to be and never had an official resident. Though Olympia was to be the place everyone wanted to live and visit, today it can only be found on a map—but not your ordinary map. Olympia is found only on old maps dating to the 1920s. The energy of Olympia can be felt when visiting the area of Hobe Sound, known as Old Hobe Sound, where Bridge Road meets up with Old Dixie Highway and the FEC tracks.

The only remnants of the city are some roads named for Greek and Roman gods, as planned by Fatio, including Mars, Athena, Apollo, Venus and Ceres. The old Olympia town hall is set on Apollo Road, which was the sales office for developers from the Olympia Improvement Corp. Several of the original buildings were purchased by Martin County and the Reed family of Jupiter Island, and the current city of Hobe Sound essentially arose from the ashes of Olympia.

Legends claim a ghost exists in the area where Olympia–Picture City was located. This spirit is that of a failed actress who killed herself on one of the sets. Several people who have visited the area and explored the ruins have reported having severe bouts of unexplainable depression and sadness.

Besides the feeling of sadness, since there is not much left of Olympia, not many people pay attention to the possibility of paranormal activity in this area of Hobe Sound.

33

PIGEON KEY

Every culture has various superstitions and legends associated with death and how sometimes death can be predicted, such as the Spanish superstition that warns when a bird sings outside your window at night, a death will occur in your home the following day.[19] Other superstitions and legends share that death leaves a calling card after it comes, including the one at the bridge tender's home in Florida's Pigeon Key.

Pigeon Key holds the truth behind a Florida legend that tells the tale of Leona Kyle, the wife of the Seven-Mile Bridge tender Robert Kyle. The two lived on the small island off Moser Channel.

Legend claims Leona was having an affair with a cook or the assistant bridge tender (stories vary). Her husband never discovered the truth behind her affair, but the legend claims she was overcome with guilt and unable to live with the burden of the shame so she climbed the stairs of their home and hanged herself from the rafter.

Those who stay overnight on the island are often awakened by the sound of a dress brushing across the floor and see mysterious lights in the windows when no one is supposed to be inside. Other paranormal accounts on the island include feeling cold chills on hot summer nights, hearing whispers and a loud thud that shakes the floor and wakes campers. Some believe that the loud thud is Leona's spirit reliving the hanging, and it is the feeling of her body hitting the floor.

Additionally, this legend is tied to a mysterious handprint that appears on some nights on the beam from which Leona hanged herself. Employees have washed and painted the beam with the handprint, but for an unknown reason, it keeps reappearing. Some people believe the handprint is her spirit reaching out for help.

This story is just a legend, and there are no supporting facts that these events are factual, just a spooky campfire story. So, if the story is just a story, why are so many people experiencing paranormal activity when visiting Pigeon Key? There are many reasons why this could be happening.

Left: Pigeon Key and the Seven Mile Bridge on the Overseas Highway to Key West, Florida. *State Archives of Florida, Florida Memory.*

Below: Aerial view showing the Overseas Highway at Pigeon Key, Florida. *State Archives of Florida, Florida Memory.*

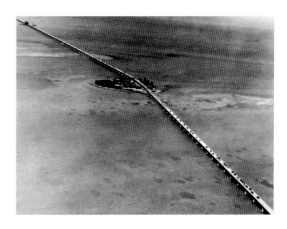

Aerial view of Pigeon Key. *State Archives of Florida, Florida Memory.*

One is the story of Laura Woodward, who was the wife of G.M. Woodward, the bridge tender for the Florida East Coast Railroad Company at Pigeon Key. She did die by suicide, shooting herself in the temple. Her husband discovered her body lying across their bed when he returned home from work in the afternoon. She left no letter explaining why she killed herself, and her husband reported his wife was suffering from depression and ill.

Many paranormal researchers believe it is Laura's spirit, not Leona haunting Pigeon Key. Some feel she remains behind because the urban legend being told is not hers, and she wants to share her story.

Like many other keys in the area, Pigeon Key suffered significant devastation during the aftermath of the 1909 hurricane. Even though much of the island was destroyed, it is still worth visiting. Because of the remoteness, not many people visit the island, which adds to the eeriness and makes it a quiet place to relax and speak with the spirits that remain behind.

Other claims of paranormal activity include seeing ghosts in the windows of houses on the island, hearing phantom trains passing by and feeling something sitting on their chest when lying down at night.

Several buildings on Pigeon Key have been restored, including a museum showcased the eccentricities of life on the island in the early twentieth century. Unfortunately, over the years, this island has been cut off from the mainland, and many refer to Pigeon Key as the ghost island of the Florida Keys.

34

QUAY

When the idea of Quay began in 1910, it was developed in honor of a local U.S. senator, Matthew Quay, from Port St. Lucie. However, the town failed to attract developers and financial backers, ending the idea of a beautiful town from becoming a reality. Before being renamed Quay, the town was known as Woodley, and then eventually, the town of Quay changed its name to Winter Beach.

Though the town never thrived like other Florida locations, there is a small cemetery, the oldest in Indian River County. Several Florida natives share stories and warn cemetery visitors that if they enter the cemetery, they will most likely have a spirit follow them home. Some have claimed the paranormal activity they experience after visiting the graveyard lasts at least one month before it stops.

In addition to the cemetery, this community has a few scattered residents, a post office and many abandoned buildings. None of the original buildings remain in Quay, but some of the old dock pilings were part of the historic roadway and wooden bridge that crossed the Intracoastal way.

Since Winter Beach is such a small part of Indian River County, those who do not know what they are looking for often drive through or past the town without knowing it. There might not be much to see or explore, but the cemetery is worth the visit, giving all visitors an insight into the community's history—and possibly a new spirit friend to bring home.

SULPHUR SPRINGS

Sulphur Springs, Florida, is a ghost town that is every paranormal researcher's dream destination. This town was once a bustling community filled with shopping, entertainment, dining and many more things for residents to enjoy. In the late 1800s, this area was a serene mineral spring enjoyed by locals and visited by many wanting a relaxing getaway.

A lighthouse once stood at the site of the Sulphur Springs Water Tower to help watch for pirates and aid ship captains navigating the Gulf of Mexico's coastline. Eventually, the lighthouse was demolished, leaving a dark spot in the area and the area's history.

Many years later, Josiah Richardson arrived in Sulphur Springs in the 1920s. Richardson was on a mission to make the area the latest and greatest tourist attraction. Since Sulphur Springs had a reputation for containing healing waters, he wanted to attract more visitors by developing the Sulphur Springs

Sulphur Springs. *Haines Photo Company, State Archives of Florida, Florida Memory.*

Hotel and Apartments. He also created the Sulphur Springs Arcade, Florida's first indoor shopping venue, on the first floor of the hotel/apartment building. Richardson had ambitious dreams, and he planned to continue adding to the resort development, including the addition of a spa and alligator farm.

The need for additional water pressure to serve the hotel and attractions required the construction of a water tower in the area. Richardson was forced to mortgage his entire resort to fund the construction of the 200,000-gallon Sulphur Springs water tower. Sadly, Richardson's dream was short-lived, and his tourist attraction venture swiftly disappeared.

In 1933, water rushed toward the Arcade and the Sulphur Springs Hotel and Apartments, causing significant damage and forcing all the shops to close. Richardson watched as his heavily mortgaged investment property was destroyed. The destruction left him bankrupt, and Sulphur Springs quickly became another one of Florida's ghost towns.

A drive-in theater was built in 1951, bringing new life to Sulphur Springs, making it a popular place to hang out and watch the latest movies. The theater constructed a neon tower mimicking the water tower, which stood over the drive-in movie theater. This movie theater was active, showing the latest movies for over forty years.

The land around the Sulphur Springs Tower experienced many transformations throughout the years. It was once planned to build a residential complex under the tower, but instead, the area remained empty until it became a community park.

As the Great Depression swept the nation, many living in the Tampa area, like others, were struggling with dire economic situations. Even the

Beach and pool at Sulphur Springs. *State Archives of Florida, Florida Memory.*

Top: Dam and overflow at Sulphur Springs, Tampa, Florida. *State Archives of Florida, Florida Memory.*

Bottom: On Hillsborough River at Sulphur Springs, Tampa, Florida. *State Archives of Florida, Florida Memory.*

wealthiest of Florida families lost their livelihoods and were left fearing their financial future.

Sadness swept through the area, and when desperation hit, several people struggling to feed their families took rash, frantic measures. Many people believed the only way they could escape the feeling of hopelessness was through the tragic act of suicide. In one year, it was reported that at least forty thousand Americans took their own lives as a result of the Great Depression. Several people in the area considered the Sulphur Springs Water Tower their only hope and an opportunity to escape the tragic fate they thought their future held. There is no exact number of how many people climbed to the top of the water tower before plummeting to their death. But one thing we do know is many spirits from those who saw jumping from the tower as their only hope remain behind, haunting the tower and the park below.

Sulphur Springs has a horrific past, including flooding, failed business adventures and suicide. It comes as no surprise that the water tower the town is known for is the place where several supernatural and eerie events occur.

Today, Sulphur Springs has large pockets of historical areas waiting to be explored and investigated. The spirits in town also wait for people to talk to them. Several visitors have reported mysterious happenings, eerie sounds and seeing apparitions fall to their death from the water tower, which replaced an old lighthouse.

Reports of ghostly activity include a man in Depression-era clothing who has been spotted wandering the top of the tower, slowly pacing back and forth. People who have witnessed this spirit feel sad when walking around the water tower.

Another spirit is of a woman spotted at the top of the water tour who abruptly jumps off the tower, plunging to her death. However, it is said that her apparition disappears right before impact. She is not the only spirit seen jumping off the tower; many have reported seeing various ghosts in different period clothing jumping off the top of the building.

The desperate spirits around the water tower are not the only spirits to haunt Sulphur Springs. The tower stands where a lighthouse once illuminated the area, helping mariners and pirates navigate the waters of the Tampa Bay area. Local legends claim a special connection between Sulphur Springs and the sea, and the lighthouse was used as a marker on an infamous treasure map.

Once the lighthouse was demolished, pirates lost their guiding light to their buried treasure. Today, the spirits of pirates have been spotted wandering around the tower in search of clues about where their hidden gem may be. Additionally, their pirate ship has been spotted aimlessly sailing on the river before slowly disappearing.

The pirates and their ship are most likely unable to rest because they continue frantically searching for their lost booty.

When driving along Florida's Interstate 275, there is a stunning white tower structure that is impressive in size and has an interesting history. The tower is a reminder of the area's tragic past and is home to many Sulphur Springs ghosts.

38

WHITE CITY

D anish settlers quickly built the town of White City based on inspiration from the 1893 Chicago World's Fair. The town seemed to appear overnight and vanished as soon as it appeared.

Set on the southern border of the city of Fort Pierce, White City was designed and constructed by Daniel Burnham. The main road going through the town center was named Midway Road after the World's Fair Midway and ran one mile, holding everything residents needed for entertainment.

For a small town, White City prospered, with many residents living happy lives in their private community. Then one day, a con man came to town, stealing many of the residents' fortunes within one year of his arrival. Colonel Myers created a money and land scam that ultimately resulted in many residents losing their homes and livelihoods. Many of these residents left the community searching for jobs and a place to rebuild their lives.

Unfortunately, the following year, a large freeze came through the area, destroying all the crops. The freezing temperatures were the final devastating event the

Church in White City, Florida. *State Archives of Florida, Florida Memory.*

White City Bridge over the Intracoastal Waterway. *State Archives of Florida, Florida Memory.*

remaining residents could endure. Shortly after, White City was completely abandoned.

More than one hundred years after the collapse of White City, several locals attempted restoration efforts to bring the town's history back to life. Many believe that the town's con man, Colonel Myers, has remained behind and his spirit now haunts the city.

Every time an attempt is made to conduct restorations in White City, the projects are mysteriously destroyed, and personal items, including tools and gold watches, disappear without a trace.

39

YEEHAW JUNCTION

Nestled along Florida State Road 60 and US 441 near the Florida Turnpike is Yeehaw Junction, a small town that became popular during a time when family road trips were starting to become popular. The most significant structure in Yeehaw Junction is the Desert Inn, built in 1898. The inn had local cattle ranchers who frequented the establishment, and it is rumored that, at one time, it served as a brothel for the local ranchers and lonely travelers.

During its peak, Yeehaw Junction was named after the Florida East Coast Railway's Kissimmee Valley Line, Yechaw Station, which passed through the town from 1915 to 1947. The city is rumored to be named after the "Yeehaw" call local cattle ranchers would make, but some believe the name is from the Creek language word for "wolf."

When it was still standing, the Desert Inn and Restaurant had several original newspaper articles on display revealing the town's original name was "Jackass Junction" or "Jackass Crossing." Historians believe this name came from the four-corner site where local ranchers rode burros to the Desert Inn during the early 1930s. This was when the site was a local brothel, and it was common to see a bunch of "jackasses" tied up outside, waiting for their owners to return.

The Florida legislature felt a name change was needed during the 1950s when the Florida Turnpike was under construction. As the turnpike's construction brought the highway through the community in 1957, politicians believed it was best to rename the town Yeehaw for travel

Yeehaw Junction today as you drive into town heading west toward the Desert Inn. *Heather Leigh.*

Desert Inn Bar and Restaurant after it was struck twice by tractor trailers. *Aidan Carroll-Landon.*

Another image of Yeehaw Junction as it stands today as you drive into town heading west from Vero Beach, Florida. *Heather Leigh.*

purposes. Otherwise, they felt too many people would continue driving by, waiting for a more welcoming town name to stop for rest, food and gas.

Though the Desert Inn was the place to go for food, drinks and a place to sleep back in the day, today the decimated remains barely stand. The building was struck twice by inattentive tractor-trailer drivers, causing significant damage to the historic structure. The first tractor-trailer accident occurred on December 22, 2019, when the driver lost control of the trailer and ran off the road, colliding with the two-story Desert Inn Bar and Restaurant structure.

The area was home to several gas stations, and slowly those rest and fueling sites became abandoned and were eventually razed. It was a popular location to stop, take a break from driving and get discounted tickets for theme parks and attractions in Orlando.

Billboards claiming "We Pay Your Toll" was the standing offer given to all travelers who stopped by the ticket booth to get their theme park and attraction tickets. The ticket booth has been shut down, billboards removed, and it no longer exists in Yeehaw Junction.

Stuckey's Pecan Shop building still stands and is now a BP station, and Pilot and Racetrac were constructed to meet the demand of Florida Turnpike travelers.

Yeehaw Junction is a working ghost town today, but you may believe it will be a completely abandoned ghost town within the next decade or two.

Several reports of paranormal activity are occurring in buildings found in Yeehaw Junction and along the lonely roads.

One ghostly story is from the Desert Inn Bar and Restaurant when upstairs was a bordello. There was a mirror believed to be original to the building, and several people have reported seeing various ghosts within the mirror's reflection. Several visitors have also reported seeing pictures move around the room on their own and rock back and forth while hanging on the walls. Though vibrations caused by a passing tractor-trailer could explain the movement of the photographs, it is still unknown what or who caused the ghostly apparitions to appear in the mirror.

Based on the various online reports, there is no doubt that the Desert Inn Bar and Restaurant are haunted by the spirits of Yeehaw Junction's past.

40

THE UNDERWATER GHOST TOWN

When most people think about ghost towns, they think about an abandoned location with many crumbling buildings. An underwater ghost town is one of the last things that comes to mind when planning to explore ghost towns in Florida.

With 18.5 percent[20] of Florida's land area covered in water, it is no surprise to learn that hidden beneath the surface of the state's most popular lake is a spooky ghost town believed to be connected to many of the area's paranormal activities.

Lake Okeechobee is a popular destination in Florida, and many tourists and locals have fallen in love with the lake and surrounding areas. Stretching over seven hundred square miles, Lake Okeechobee is one of the best places in Florida to go fishing and vacation. But only a few who explore the lake area know of the hidden town beneath the surface of the second-largest body of freshwater in the United States.

Hundreds (if not thousands) of ghost sightings, unexplained activity and strange occurrences are reported around Lake Okeechobee annually—everything from ancient monsters living in the lake to spirits lurking on the water's surface. Many who have experienced paranormal activity when visiting the lake believe Lake Okeechobee is one of the most haunted locations in Florida. So what is this underwater ghost town beneath the surface of Lake Okeechobee?

Several theories explain why so many bodies were laid to rest in this portion of the lake. One is that this is the final resting site of thousands of people who are believed to have lost their lives during a massive hurricane. According to local legend, it is also possible that the skeletons are members of the Seminole tribes who lived in the area and died from famine, war and disease. Another theory is that the bodies are from ancient tribes dating back to the 1700s who occupied the area long before the Seminoles existed.

In the early 1900s, the southernmost portion of the lake dried up more than usual. The receding waters revealed the underwater ghost town of graves, including hundreds of skeletons lying in the lakebed. However, no one knows the complete history behind why these bodies were set on the bottom of the lake and why they remain there.

41

MORE FLORIDA GHOST TOWNS

As mentioned, Florida is home to more than 250 ghost towns, many of which are extremely haunted. Several other ghost towns in Florida offer many opportunities to dive deep into Florida's past. Even though there are no significant reports of paranormal activity, it doesn't mean these towns aren't haunted. Some of the state's most significant ghost towns have an eerie presence and make for some of the best vacations and explorations. The following ghost towns do not have any significant paranormal claims but are famous and worth researching.

Ellaville

Ellaville was one of the most popular towns in Suwannee County, Florida, and many businesses set up shop in the community. Ellaville was home to sawmills, logging companies, railroad building companies and turpentine manufacturers. Back in the 1800s, Ellaville was the community to move to if someone was looking for employment. Struck by racial hate crimes, Ellaville quickly became unsafe, and many residents left town. When local structures, including homes, were attacked and burned to the ground, the remaining residents left town, seeking a safer community.

Hall City

A preacher from Chicago came to Florida and attempted to build the town of Hall City, but unfortunately, the town never took off. Set in Glades County, the community was home to about one hundred people and remained isolated from nearby villages. With no jobs, residents had no reason to stay and the 1920s abandoned Hall City.

Kismet

Nestled in the Ocala National Forest, Kismet is a Lake County ghost town. Founded in 1884, Kismet was a citrus town and was one of the locations during the late 1800s where the St. John's and Eustis Railroad had planned an extension of the railway. However, the Great Freeze in Florida destroyed most citrus crops, driving many residents out of town.

Though nothing shows what life in Kismet was like, it remains a popular ghost town because it was where Elias Disney and his wife, Flora Call, were married on New Year's Day 1888. Walt Disney, their son, visited Kismet often as a child.

Acron

Acron is another ghost town in Lake County that has become famous because of its relation to Walt Disney. The city was established during the late nineteenth century and is where the Disneys, with their children Walt and Roy O., lived for a short time. Elias and Flora are buried in the Ponceannah Cemetery near Paisley.

Bean City

Bean City was a booming farming community in Palm Beach County, and many residents made their living growing and cultivating string beans. The hurricane of 1928 destroyed the farms and many of the structures in Bean City, leaving this ghost town another abandoned community in Florida.

Flamingo

Nestled on the southern tip of the Florida Everglades is a beautiful ghost town with a significant population of pink flamingos.

At the turn of the twentieth century, Flamingo was a popular vacation destination, and despite being challenging to live in, many people loved living in the isolated community. Several years later, the population started to dwindle, and several abandoned buildings remained standing until they became significantly damaged by Hurricane Wilma in 2005.

Pine Level

The Sarasota Gang came to Pine Level in DeSoto County, making this small town their headquarters. Like a scene from a Wild West movie, this town was subjected to gunfights, gambling, drinking and prostitution. The Pine Level Methodist Church is the only remaining structure in this eerie ghost town today.

Slavia

Settled by immigrants from Slovakia, Slavia was a town built for industrial workers wanting to raise their children on quiet farms, far from the wickedness of large cities. The Holy Trinity Slovak Lutheran Church bought 1,200 acres for $17,400 to create their new hometown of Slavia. Since the 1920s, Slavia has been completely abandoned, with only a few glimpses into the town's history via a Florida Historical Marker.

Sisco

Today, Sisco is almost completely deserted but was once a community founded by a colony of Seventh-day Adventists. The Great Freeze destroyed much of the area's vegetation; without food, many of the residents packed up and left town. Some descendants of Reverend Main served the city, living in this quiet and eerie ghost town.

Zion

Set along the East Coast of Florida in Palm Beach County, Zion had a unique history and some rumors of being haunted. There was a small house used to house refugees that burned down in 1927. Zion also had a small post office, which was discontinued in 1892. Since the house burned down, several residents fled the area, putting Zion on the list of Florida ghost towns.

Romeo

Built in the 1850s, Romeo was a farming town in Marion County. This town is interesting because most local farmers mysteriously disappeared, and no one knows what happened to them or where they went.

NOTES

1. "What Is a Ghost Town? WMH Town Classifications Explained," Western Mining History, https://westernmininghistory.com/664/what-is-a-ghost-town-wmh-town-classifications-explained/.
2. Toni Collins, "Cedar Key News: Seahorse Key's Haunting History," Cedar Key News, https://cedarkeynews.com/Archives/OLDSITE/Features/291-315.html.
3. "Balm—Ghost Town," Ghost Towns, https://www.ghosttowns.com/states/fl/balm.html.
4. "10 Most Terrifying Haunted Bike Trails in Florida," Backpackerverse, December 13, 2016, https://backpackerverse.com/best-bike-trails-in-florida/.
5. Dan Asfar, *Ghost Stories of Florida* (Edmonton: Lone Pine Publishing, 2005).
6. "Zachary Taylor | the Zachary Taylor Project," ZTP, https://www.thezacharytaylorproject.com/zachary-taylor.
7. Editors, "President Zachary Taylor Dies Unexpectedly," History, https://www.history.com/this-day-in-history/president-zachary-taylor-dies-unexpectedly.
8. "Fort Basinger, Florida – Ghost Town on the Kissimmee River," Legends of America, https://www.legendsofamerica.com/fort-basinger-florida/.
9. "History of BulowVille | Florida State Parks." Florida State Parks, https://www.floridastateparks.org/learn/history-bulowville.
10. Ellen Sturm Niz, "The Spookiest Ghost Towns in America," Country Living, October 11, 2019, https://www.countryliving.com/life/travel/g2665/spookiest-ghost-towns-in-america/.
11. Sisco Deen, "Espanola," Flagler County Historical Society, October 16, 2019, https://flaglercountyhistoricalsociety.com/espanola/.

12. "History of Egmont Key | Florida State Parks," Florida State Parks, July 12, 2023, https://www.floridastateparks.org/learn/history-egmont-key.

13. ABC7 Staff, "May 9 Marks 43rd Anniversary of Sunshine Skyway Bridge Collapse," ABC7, May 9, 2023, https://www.mysuncoast.com/2023/05/09/may-9-marks-43rd-anniversary-sunshine-skyway-bridge-collapse/.

14. "Fort Jefferson—Dry Tortugas National Park," National Park Service, https://www.nps.gov/drto/learn/historyculture/fort-jefferson.htm.

15. "Fort Pickens—Gulf Islands National Seashore," Visit Pensacola, https://www.visitpensacola.com/directory/fort-pickens-gulf-islands-national-seashore/.

16. "Judah P. Benjamin Confederate Memorial at Gamble Plantation Historic State Park | Florida State Parks," Florida State Parks, https://www.floridastateparks.org/parks-and-trails/judah-p-benjamin-confederate-memorial-gamble-plantation-historic-state-park.

17. Brad Bertelli, "Keys History: Survivors of Attack at Indian Key Detail Horrifying Carnage," *Florida Keys Weekly Newspapers*, August 9, 2021, https://keysweekly.com/42/keys-history-survivors-of-attack-at-indian-key-detail-horrifying-carnage/.

18. "Heartbreak Hotel," Atlas Obscura, https://www.atlasobscura.com/places/heartbreak-hotel.

19. David Sloan, "The Mysterious Handprint at Pigeon Key," *Florida Keys Weekly Newspapers*, October 29, 2019, https://keysweekly.com/42/the-mysterious-handprint-at-pigeon-key/.

20. "How Wet Is Your State? The Water Area of Each State," U.S. Geological Survey, https://www.usgs.gov/special-topics/water-science-school/science/how-wet-your-state-water-area-each-state.

BIBLIOGRAPHY

Abandoned Florida. "Fort Dade." May 20, 2014. https://www.abandonedfl.com.

Allen, Rick. "Florida Ghost Towns." *Gainesville Sun*, October 20, 2013. https://www.gainesville.com.

Backpackerverse. "These 10 Florida Ghost Towns Are the Perfect Ghost Hunting Destinations." https://backpackerverse.com.

Balzano, Christopher. *Haunted Florida Love Stories*. Charleston, SC: The History Press, 2020.

Caporale, Patricia. "Eldora Echoes with Whispers of Thriving Past." *Orlando Sentinel*, November 12, 1992.

Carlson, Charlie. *Weird Florida*. New York: Sterling Publishing, 2009.

Coleman, Lynn. "Tidbits about the Old Brick Road in Florida." Heroes, Heroines and History. August 28, 2014. https://www.hhhistory.com.

Coullias, Lynn. "Hague, Florida: A Walk Through History" (PDF). Alachua County Board of Commissioners. June 10, 2014.

Federal Writers' Project. "Lee, Robert E. A Letter Regarding the Reservation of the Florida Keys for Military Forces." In *A Guide to the Southernmost State*, 206. New York: Oxford University Press, 1939.

Florida State Parks. "Camp Helen State Park | Florida State Parks." www.floridastateparks.org.

———. "Indian Key Historic State Park." https://www.floridastateparks.org.

———. "Koreshan State Park." https://www.floridastateparks.org.

Ghost Towns. "Anona—Ghost Town." www.ghosttowns.com.

————. "Ghost Towns of Florida." www.ghosttowns.com.

Island Hotel & Restaurant. "Island Hotel Ghost Stories." https://www.islandhotel-cedarkey.com.

Jenkins, Greg. *Florida's Ghostly Legends and Haunted Folklore*. Lanham, MD: Rowman & Littlefield, 2013.

Kite-Powell, Rodney. "Pirates, Real and Legendary, Left Their Mark on the Tampa Area." *Tampa Tribune*, June 16, 2014.

Lechner, Dinah Marie. "Kerr City." *Ocala StarBanner*, January 30, 2006. https://www.ocala.com.

Leigh, Heather. *Haunted Southern Nevada Ghost Towns*. Charleston, SC: The History Press, 2022.

Mahon, John K. *History of the Second Seminole War, 1835–1842*. Gainesville: Library Press at the University of Florida, 2017.

Miller, Mike. "Espanola, Florida Old Brick Road." Florida Back Roads Travel. August 22, 2023.

————. "Florida Ghost Towns." Florida Back Roads Travel. July 4, 2023. https://www.florida-backroads-travel.com.

Moore, Roger. "Doris Leeper Was a 'Force for the Arts.'" *Orlando Sentinel*, April 12, 2000.

My Panhandle. "Camp Helen State Park Rumored to Be Home to Ghosts." www.mypanhandle.com.

Naples Florida Travel Guide. "Koreshan State Park: The Hollow Earth History of Estero Florida." September 14, 2022. https://www.naplesfloridatravelguide.com.

National Park Service. "Eldora—Canaveral National Seashore (U.S. National Park Service)." www.nps.gov.

Nightly Spirits "The Sulphur Springs Water Tower—Haunted Tampa—Nightly Spirits." July 17, 2020. https://nightlyspirits.com.

Palm Beach Post. "See What's Left of Hollywood Ghost Town 'Picture City' in Hobe Sound." March 10, 2017. https://www.palmbeachpost.com.

Palm Coast and the Flagler Beaches. "Explore Bulow Plantation, An Eerie Ghost Town in Palm Coast and the Flagler Beaches." *Visit Flagler*. www.visitflagler.com

Pino, Mark. "Ghostly Tales Lurk within County's Past." *Orlando Sentinel*, October 29, 2006. https://www.orlandosentinel.com.

Reid, Thomas. *America's Fortress: A History of Fort Jefferson*. Gainesville: University Press of Florida, 2006.

Roman, Marisa. "Florida Has a Lost Town Most People Don't Know About." Only in Your State. August 16, 2018. https://www.onlyinyourstate.com.

———. "Most People Have No Idea There's an Underwater Ghost Town Hiding in Florida." Only in Your State. January 13, 2023. www.onlyinyourstate.com.

Rountree, Bob. "Future of Historic Desert Inn after Crash Uncertain." Florida Rambler. October 22, 2021. www.floridarambler.com.

Sanchez, Kellie. 2019. "Meet the Ghosts of Camp Helen State Park." WJHG7. October 30, 2019. https://www.wjhg.com.

Schlenker, Dave. "Fort King Site More Than Just Prankster Ghosts." *Ocala StarBanner*, March 7, 2013. https://www.ocala.com.

Trail of Florida's Indian Heritage. "Indian Key Historic State Park." https://www.trailoffloridasindianheritage.org.

Viele, John. *The Wreckers*. Lanham, MD: Rowman & Littlefield, 2013.

Visit St. Lucie Florida. "White City, FL: History, Shopping & Things to Do." https://visitstlucie.com.

Walters, Quincy. "Koreshan Ghosts Tell the Tale of Their Utopian Community." WGCU PBS & NPR for Southwest Florida. January 31, 2018. https://news.wgcu.org.

About the Author

Heather Leigh, PhD.

Heather Leigh Carroll-Landon, PhD, started her journey in the paranormal field as a teenager after multiple interactions with her grandfather, who passed away many years before. She has researched and traveled to locations to learn more about the history of the land, buildings and local area and paranormal claims. As long as she has been interested in the supernatural, Heather Leigh has been a freelance writer, writing for several newspapers, magazines and online publications. She and her family (Exploration Paranormal) appeared in Real Haunts: Ghost Towns and Real Haunts 3, where they explored many southern Nevada ghost towns and she has appeared on Ghost Adventures: Lake of Death.

She is an author of articles and books and a lecturer about all things paranormal. Her first book, *Haunted Southern Nevada Ghost Towns*, was published by The History Press in August 2022 and her second book, *Ghosts and Legends of the Vegas Valley*, was also published by The History Press in February 2023. These books were followed by her most recent book, *Haunted Florida Lighthouses*, published in September 2023. She has many more book ideas in the works and hopes to bring them to life in the near future.

She holds a Doctor of Philosophy degree in Metaphysical and Humanistic Science with a specialty in Paranormal Science. She is a Certified Paranormal

Investigator and a Certified EVP Technician. She aims to help others take a more scientific approach to paranormal investigations and research.

Heather Leigh is a co-host and content contributor for *Touch of Magick*, a podcast about magick and the supernatural. Heather Leigh is also the founder of Exploration Paranormal and co-founder of the Witches Paranormal Society. She hosts Exploring the Paranormal and is the co-host of Passport to the Paranormal with Joe Franke and co-hosts Ghost Education 101 vodcasts on Facebook and YouTube. You can find Heather Leigh on Facebook (@DrHeatherLeigh), where you will find additional information, including upcoming classes, lectures and more. Or via her websites, www. heatherleighphd.com and www.explorationparanormal.com.